WITHDRAWN

Culinary Herbs

for SHORT-SEASON

Gardeners

D1532891

The Herb Garden, Almonte, Ontario, Canada.

Culinary Herbs

for SHORT-SEASON

Gardeners

ERNEST SMALL / GRACE DEUTSCH

MOUNTAIN PRESS PUBLISHING COMPANY
Missoula, Montana / 2002

© 2001 National Research Council of Canada & Ismant Associates Inc.
All rights reserved

First co-published in Canada in 2001 by NRC Research Press and Ismant
Peony Press. Ismant Peony Press is an imprint of Ismant Associates Inc.

Mountain Press Edition, March 2002

Photograph Credits
Sharon and Gerry Channer: pages ii, x, 27, 42, 100, 101, 169
Debbie Luce: page ix
Eric Johnson: pages 28, 60, 134
Schamel First Bavarian Horseradish Delicatessen Factory: page 94

Special Illustration Credits
Barry Flahey: pages 9, 10, 13, 15, 16, 19, 21, 26, 62, 82, 99, 123 (top)
Susan Rigby and Brenda Brookes: pages 88, 89, 123 (bottom)

Library of Congress Cataloging-in-Publication Data
Small, Ernest, 1940–
   Culinary herbs for short-season gardeners / Ernest Small, Grace Deutsch.
      p. cm.
   Includes bibliographical references (p.) and index.
   ISBN 0-87842-453-9 (alk. paper)
      1. Herb gardening—Canada. 2. Herb gardening—United States. 3. Herbs—Canada.
   4. Herbs—Unites States. I. Deutsch, Grace. II. Title.

SB351.H5 S63 2002
635'.7—dc21   2002020894

PRINTED IN HONG KONG BY MANTEC PRODUCTION COMPANY

Mountain Press Publishing Company
P.O. Box 2399 • Missoula, Montana 59806
(406) 728-1900

Contents

Culinary Herb Compendium   27

A heavenly lesson in herb cultivation

Acknowledgments

Our special thanks to Sharon and Gerry Channer of the Herb Garden, Almonte, Ontario, for the use of several beautiful photographs; Debbie Luce of Herbs for All Seasons for the excellent photograph of pot marigold; Eric Johnson (photographer), Barry Flahey (artist), Susan Rigby (artist), and Brenda Brookes (technician and artist), all of Agriculture Canada, for preparing additional superb illustrations; the Schamel First Bavarian Horseradish Delicatessen Factory, Baiersdorf, Germany, for a wonderful photograph of horseradish; Marc Favreau, for excellent suggestions that clarified the text; and the staff at NRC Research Press. Most of the drawings are modified from masterpieces of botanical illustration produced in the 18th and 19th centuries that are so valuable they are kept in secure collections generally unavailable for public viewing. We trust our resurrection of their works would have pleased the artists.

Disclaimer

The information in this book has been carefully researched and all efforts have been made to ensure accuracy. The traditional medical and folk uses and modern medicinal values of the culinary herbs described here are given for informational purposes only. Medicinal use of herbs should be carried out only under the care of a well-informed, qualified physician. Do not consume or use medicinally any plant or herb unless it has been correctly identified. The authors and publishers disclaim any liability in connection with the use of the information contained in this book. Where trade names are used, no discrimination is intended and no endorsement by the authors or publishers is implied.

To

Victor, Sara, Esther, Sharon, and Karen

ES

To

Jessica, "Queen of Basil," Meara, "Precious Poppy,"

and Julia, "Princess Rose"

GD

Some fragrant, tasty herbal delights - pretty nasturtium flowers and herbal vinegars and liqueurs.

INTRODUCTION

short-season gardener *n*. Optimist who grows plants in an area with summers that are too short and winters that are too cold.

Before I met Ernie Small, I had never thought much about the basic problem inherent in growing culinary herbs in my cool-climate garden. Most herbs are native to southern climates, so they resent—at least a little, and sometimes a lot—being required to thrive in a place they find downright chilly.

I should have known better. I grew up in semi-tropical Australia, and 30 years after I emigrated to Southern Ontario, I am still grumbling about short summers and endless winters. I really admire my gardening friends in places like windswept Montana, the frigid Adirondacks, and bracing northern Alberta, who persist in creating an annual bounty of flowers, vegetables and herbs. They have learned, often through hard-won experience, that many delectable herbs can be coddled into ignoring their warm-climate origins. These resourceful gardeners exploit the relatively short warm-weather season and encourage a wonderful array of herbs into prospering in difficult, often harsh environments.

Dr. Small understands their enthusiasm and persistence. He was raised by immigrant parents in the Ottawa Valley, a region known for its short searing summers and seemingly endless winters. Ernie's parents got their start in Canada peddling fruit and vegetables from a horse-drawn cart, progressing to owning and operating grocery stores and restaurants. From a young age, Ernie was "volunteered" to help out in the family enterprises, and so unwittingly acquired an appreciation for food plants. But he had little real interest in plants of any kind until he casually took a course in biology just as he was finishing his undergraduate general arts degree. Thanks to his wonderfully inspirational teacher, he fell in love with botany.

Several decades later, Ernie is an international authority on agriculturally important plants. Winner of the G. M. Cooley Award of the American Society of Plant Taxonomists, the Southern California Botanists Prize, the Agriculture Canada Merit Award, and the prestigious Canadian Botanical Association's George Lawson Medal for lifetime contributions to botany, Ernie has written over 200 scientific publications. He has also written 7 books, including *Culinary Herbs*, the professional herb-grower's bible.

As a botanist, Ernie is interested in all classes of plants. But the idea that some plants can be beautiful and edible at the same time has always intrigued him, hence his particular interest in culinary herbs. Great chefs know that food must be simultaneously attractive to the eye, palate, and nose, and since herbs epitomize this combination of beauty, taste, and aroma, Ernie finds them ideal subjects for botanical study.

By the way, never let anyone tell you that botany is boring: while collecting herbs in Turkey, Israel, Greece, Spain, Italy, France, England, Russia and throughout North America, Ernie has risked life and limb trying to get at plants that insist on growing on steep cliffs that sensible mountain goats would not visit, had occasion to dodge snakes and/or scorpions, talked fast when faced with suspicious locals pointing guns, and reassured gimlet-eyed police who were unaware that he is also one of the world's top authorities on *Cannabis sativa*, the marijuana plant.

I met Ernie by chance at a summer herb fair. Gardeners being approachable types, we got into a lively discussion on the best basil to go with a freshly picked tomato. You know that evocative smell that transfers from the tomato to your hands, the sweet-but-acid taste, the warmth of that edible goodness … Is it 'Mammoth' (*O. basilicum*), one of the many "lettuce-leaved" cultivars, or 'Spicy Globe,' that fragrant, delectable hybrid of American basil (*O. americanum*) that crowns the tomato-lover's moments of summer ecstasy? We could not agree, although we did concur that basil was indeed "the king of herbs." Ernie did admit to a certain prejudice … there wasn't a basil he didn't like with the exception of holy basil, which he said was the worst herb he had ever tasted. (He hastened to say that perhaps this judgment was unfair since holy basil suffers by comparison to its wonderful relative.) As I knew nothing about holy basil and did not wish to advertise my ignorance, I deftly steered the conversation to dill, a particular favorite of mine, and then we parted.

My curiosity piqued about the infamous holy basil, I made for the book display area, determined to do a little unobtrusive sleuthing. At the NRC Research Press stand I discovered a very large, authoritative-looking work entitled *Culinary Herbs*. Surely I'd find all I needed to know on holy basil in this hefty book? I was just thumbing through the index, when a familiar friendly voice said: "I think holy basil is on page 419."

From basil to books was not a great leap. I told Ernie that I was endlessly on the lookout for a practical, easy-to-use book on what herbs to grow in our chilly climate, and how to grow them successfully, short hot summers and long cold winters notwithstanding. True, there are lots of books on how to grow herbs, but I don't want to be tortured with lyrical descriptions on how to grow chilli peppers and saffron crocus, when my own experiences tell me that nature and climate will always conspire against me raising these plants through to harvest. While Ernie's big book *Culinary Herbs* was obviously *the* definitive book on the subject, its size and the depth of the treatment of the 125 herb species it covers, meant it was just too hefty to be the take-to-the-garden herb book I was looking for. Ernie wondered why I did not write the book I wanted myself; I said I would, only if he would.

Timing, as they say, is everything. With his latest book *Canadian Medicinal Crops*, co-authored with his colleague Dr. Paul Catling, just completed, I had found Ernie between projects.

Moreover, he had long wanted to write a book on herbs that would put his specialist's knowledge at the service of keen amateur herb growers. And being a dirt-under-the-nails gardener himself, we found we were in total agreement that our book would not be for armchair gardeners, but for that hardy breed who, like us, wants to experience the boundless satisfaction of growing and harvesting herbs if not year-round, then as close to it as possible.

The resulting book, *Culinary Herbs for Short-Season Gardeners*, you hold in your hands. We hope you turn to it constantly as you tend your northern herb garden. (Do not be afraid to get it dirty. Like a favorite cookbook, it should testify to its usefulness by being not a little stained and dog-eared.) As the story of this book's conception indicates, gardeners like to share their knowledge. In this spirit, we would welcome receiving information on successful (and not so successful) strategies you have used in your own short-season herb garden. Please feel free to write to us c/o Ismant Peony Press, 633 Huron Street, Toronto, ON Canada M5R 2R8.

Grace Deutsch

How to Use This Book
Whether you are a novice or an experienced short-season gardener, you will get maximum benefit from this book if you take the time to read the sections that precede the "Culinary Herb Compendium," which starts on page 27.

Interpreting a Plant Hardiness Zone Map will help you determine which perennial herbs are hardy enough to survive winters in your area.

Making the Most of the Short Growing Season is full of practical advice on how to get the growing season for your herbs started early and how to keep it going late, despite the weather.

Growing and Caring for Your Herbs is a gardening primer for herb growers, covering indoor and outdoor seeding, soil for seeds and seedlings, watering and thinning, lighting requirements, transplanting indoors and outdoors, hardening off, spring and fall frost dates, preparing for winter, and mulching and wrapping perennials for winter survival.

The Culinary Herb Compendium includes more than 50 species, featuring over 100 cultivars. The herbs are arranged alphabetically by their common name. To avoid any confusion, each herb's botanical name is also included, along with the name of the plant family to which the herb belongs. A square green icon clearly marked "Annual" offsets annuals from perennials. A colored "Coldest Tolerated" zone box appears at the top of each perennial entry. The numbers given in these boxes tie in to the plant hardiness zones shown on the climatic zone map on page 6, as do the colors of the actual boxes. The boxes enable you to see instantly the coldest zone in which the herb may be expected to overwinter outdoors successfully.

The individual herb listings include the following elements:

DESCRIPTION
Gives you full information on the herb's origin; life cycle (annual, biennial, or perennial); size at maturity; leaf shape, color, taste and fragrance; stem and root formation; flowering habit;

suitability for growing in pots or containers; which parts of the plant are edible; plus any additionally desirable features, for example, if the flowers are very alluring to honeybees or butterflies.

CULTIVATION NOTES
Everything you need to know about the plant's soil, light, and moisture needs; how, when, and where to seed; seed germination times; other propagation techniques; thinning, transplanting, and spacing requirements; pest and disease problems; indoor growing instructions, where applicable; outdoor overwintering survival strategies.

HARVESTING NOTES
Tells you when and how to harvest the different parts of the plant for maximum flavor, and how best to preserve the herb for later use.

CULINARY USES
Provides an eye-opening range of culinary uses, both domestic and commercial, for the herb, along with guidance on when it should be added in the cooking process. If the herb makes a refreshing tea, brewing instructions are given.

CRAFT USES
Gives suggestions for enjoying the herb's natural beauty.

MEDICINAL USES
Details the plant's uses in traditional herbal medicine and its value, if any, in modern medicine and pharmaceutical products. Also provides valuable nutritional information about the herb.

CAUTIONS
Offers information on existing known problems that susceptible individuals may experience from consumption of or contact with the herb.

CULTIVARS AND RELATIVES
Gives a descriptive listing of other useful plants related to the herb, plus outstanding cultivars.

HERBAL TRIVIA
As humans have ascribed wondrous powers to herbs since antiquity, we have included in each listing in the Compendium snippets of the myths, legends, and folklore that surround each herb. We found these bits of herbal trivia fascinating, and hope you will, too.

*I*NTERPRETING A PLANT HARDINESS ZONE MAP

Whether you are a novice or an experienced short-season gardener, consulting a plant hardiness zone map will help you to determine which perennial herbs are sufficiently hardy to survive winters in your area.

The plant hardiness zone map for North America shown on page 6 is a modification of a widely used climate-zone map prepared by the US Department of Agriculture. This map, which is based on minimum winter temperatures, divides the United States and Canada into climate zones, of which zones 1 through 10 are shown in the map. Each climate zone is divided from the next by a difference of 5.6°C (10°F). Lower zone numbers indicate lower minimum winter temperatures.

Each of the perennial herbs profiled in the "Culinary Herb Compendium" includes a reference to the coldest zone tolerated by the plant. To find out whether a particular herb may be winter-hardy enough for your location, look at the map to find your gardening area. Then match the map color for your location to the map key to determine the hardiness zone you live in. Note, however, that the hardiness zone listings are based on general temperature trends. Neither the hardiness zone map nor the plant hardiness listings necessarily reflects the conditions peculiar to your garden or your immediate area. You may find, for example, that you can grow a particular herb a zone north of its stated maximum limit simply by varying its microclimate, that is, the climate in the plant's immediate vicinity.

Local factors, such as the amount of snow cover, can also alter the significance of minimum winter temperatures. Snow cover decreases the extent that frost penetrates into the ground, so if you live in an area with consistently heavy snow, your garden may be warmer, from a plant's perspective, than the hardiness zone map would indicate. Conversely, if you live in an area that experiences mid-winter thaws that melt the snow cover, you may be warmer, but the range of herbs you can grow will be more limited compared to those areas where snow stays all winter.

Finally, hardiness zones should not be considered to be sharp like political boundaries, as this could lead to the absurd prediction that the south side of some gardens bisected by the map lines could grow some herbs that could not be grown on the north side.

Given the limitations of hardiness zone maps, you may wonder why you should be especially concerned about plant hardiness listings. While you can do much to help your outdoor herbs survive the cold season, you can only compensate for minimum winter temperatures to a limited extent. And while minimum winter temperature alone is probably not sufficient to predict a plant's hardiness limits, it remains the most important factor in determining whether a perennial species will survive in a given region. So do treat plant hardiness listings as flexible guidelines, but know that there simply is not a better predictive system at present.

Plant hardiness zone map for North America. Culinary Herbs for Short-Season Gardeners *is aimed primarily at gardeners cultivating herbs in zones 1–5.*

MAKING THE MOST OF THE SHORT GROWING SEASON

Cultivating culinary herbs in a northern climate is a challenge. The outdoor growing season is short and intense, and climatic conditions—even in the summer months—are notoriously fickle. The bad news is that you can't do anything about the climate. The good news is that there is much you can do to get the growing season for your herbs started early and to keep it going late, despite the weather.

Pick the Best Location for Light and Warmth

Although many culinary herbs are Mediterranean and/or Asian natives, a number grow well in cold-climate gardens, albeit as annuals rather than perennials, which they may well be in warmer, long-season climates. (Annual herbs like dill, mustard, and coriander last only one growing season and must be replanted each year. Perennials like fennel, lemon balm, and Oriental poppy reappear in the spring after wintering outdoors.)

Light is crucial for most herbs. Whether grown as annuals or perennials, many herbs require a minimum of 6 hours of direct sunlight daily in order to thrive. So when you're deciding where to grow your herbs, pick those locations that have maximum light potential. Sites with a southern or southeastern aspect that catch the morning sun will be best for most culinary herbs, as these exposures will provide your herbs with the greatest amount of light (and warmth) for the longest period of time, from sunrise to mid-afternoon.

Meeting your herbs' need for warmth is another consideration when choosing suitable garden sites. Providing warmth is always important, but it's especially so during spring when you're working feverishly to give young seedlings a good start on the season, and conversely, in fall, when you're counting on harvesting a late crop. House and garden walls made of brick retain the day's heat and radiate it at night, so making a herb garden in front of a wall ensures warmth and has the added benefit of sheltering your plants from damaging winds. Plant shorter herbs at the front of your bed, reserving the wall position for taller herbs like angelica or lovage that are always in need of support. Alternatively, erecting a sturdy trellis in front of a sunny wall allows climbing herbs like hops and certain types of nasturtiums to ramble at will, in the process helping to soften the wall's harsh contours.

Walkways and paths made of stone or brick also retain precious heat. Growing herbs beside a garden path helps keep the plants warm and gives you easy access for harvesting herbs for fresh use whenever you need them. Because herbs like garlic chives and sweet marjoram are both fragrant and pretty, they make delightful borders as well. Other sources of warmth your garden may have to offer include ornamental rocks and rock gardens.

Full Sun Versus Full Sun/Partial Shade

Different herbs have different light needs. The "Cultivation Notes" for each herb profiled in the "Culinary Herb Compendium" will tell you what light conditions the plant requires.

- *Full sun* means the plant should be in a location where it can receive a minimum of 6 hours of direct sunlight each day and at least filtered light for the rest of the day. (Filtered light is light that is screened by the leafy branches of nearby trees or shrubs.)
- *Full sun/partial shade* means the plant should be in a location where it can receive at least 4 hours of direct sunshine a day, but either tolerates or does best with filtered sunshine or shade for the rest of the day.

Provide Wind Protection and Cold Air Drainage

Plants lose moisture to evaporation through their leaves, so herbs that are buffeted by harsh winds will find the effects very drying indeed. Windbreaks can modify the damage caused by drying cold winds. A good windbreak cuts down on the effect of the wind, but doesn't block it entirely. The standard solid upright wooden fence that encloses many backyard gardens makes a poor windbreak as it only serves to channel the force of the wind in another direction, with probably even greater force. A perforated fence, which is constructed by staggering the spaces between each upright, does allow some of the wind to blow through, but it's a more gentle wind that reaches your plants. Perforated fences also promote ventilation, let more light into your garden, and let cold air pass out. Existing hedges and shrubs can also act as windbreaks. You can also buy readymade windbreak fences, or make less permanent structures by stretching windbreak netting or burlap between poles.

Herbs will suffer if left to sit in pockets of cold air, particularly at night when frosts can occur only in the pockets. Since cold air moves downward, you want to design your herb garden so that it has a slight slope, assuming there is no natural slope on your land that you can take advantage of. Sloping gardens promote cold air drainage; however, as the cold air will collect at the bottom of the slope, be careful not to plant more tender herbs such as basil in this spot. Sloping gardens may have the added benefit of providing pockets of warmth, as plants growing higher up the slope block the flow of cold air reaching those plants situated immediately below. The downside is that the blocked air may create a cold pocket just above the "protective" plants.

There are a number of techniques you can use to provide your herbs with adequate warmth. Try to situate your garden where it will benefit from the maximum sunlight and, by extension, the maximum heat that comes with a southern exposure. If your budget allows, an attached greenhouse with a southern exposure is useful for starting herbs early in the season. As brick house walls and stone or brick walkways retain heat, growing your herbs beside these structures provides the plants with warmth, even when the temperature drops at night. Designing your garden so that it slopes away from the plantings beside the house allows cold air to drain away at night. A perforated or picket fence makes an excellent barrier to the cooling and drying effects of strong winds (shown here by the arrow), while still allowing ventilation for your garden.

Build Raised Beds for Warmth and Drainage

Garden beds come in 2 basic kinds: those at ground level and those that are raised above ground level. For the short-season gardener, raised beds have several advantages over ground-level beds. Raised beds provide better drainage for your herbs than ground-level beds. Good drainage is vital because even the hardiest herb won't survive long in heavy, soggy soil, which promotes the growth of those micro-organisms that cause root diseases. Well-drained soil helps the plants' roots to withstand the effects of heavy rains and snow runoff. The soil in raised beds warms up more quickly in the spring than the soil in regular ground-level garden beds. This is because the beds are situated above the ground and so are surrounded by air on all sides. The wood, stone, or brick sides of the bed also act as heat retainers. Raised beds require less work to look well tended because the growing area is contained, and as the beds can be built to suit individual height requirements, you'll find that working a raised bed is decidedly easier on your back. Raised beds are ideal for seniors or physically challenged gardeners as the beds can be built high enough to allow for cultivating while standing, or from a wheelchair.

Plants grown in raised garden beds have a head start on those cultivated in ground-level beds. This is because the ground is naturally cool, and warms very slowly, while raised beds heat up with the sun much more quickly. Raised bed walls made of brick absorb and retain heat particularly well. To minimize back strain, build your raised beds to suit your particular height requirements. A masonry walkway abutting the bed makes for easier access.

Raised beds are usually about 1 m (3 feet) wide, allowing the gardener easy access to both sides of the bed. Length is less important and can depend on how much space you wish to dedicate to your herb garden. You'll need wood, brick, or stone to build the walls of your bed. Wood is likely the easiest and cheapest to acquire, as you can use rough lumber. (To prolong the life of a wooden frame, use cedar, or use preserved wood but line the walls with sturdy plastic sheeting to prevent the plants from contacting the toxic preservative.) Use string to mark off the boundaries of your bed. Raise the soil in your planting area into a mound and build your frame around it. If you're breaking new ground for your raised bed, you need to remove the existing sod. If your raised bed is going to be relatively low, say 30 cm (12 inches) high, cover the gardening area with newspapers to keep weeds at bay. Anchor the newspaper with small rocks. Build your frame and fill it with a mix of compost and friable, that is, crumbly, soil. (A mix of 2 parts topsoil, 1 part garden sand, and 1 part compost works well for most herbs.) Follow the same procedure for higher frames, omitting the newspaper layer as the increased volume of earth should suppress any ground-level weeds.

Choose the Right Species
Herb catalogs, whether print or online, are both a delight and a source of frustration to short-season gardeners. So many tantalizing herbs to choose from, so many that just won't survive in our gardens. (If you're on the lookout for herb catalogs, check the "Sources" section on page 174.) Herb catalogs indicate whether a plant is an annual, a biennial, or a perennial. (Biennial plants have to survive a winter or at least a given period of low temperatures before they can produce seeds.) Catalogs usually provide plant hardiness zone listings for all the seeds and plants that they carry.

Whether you decide to buy seeds or plants, selecting herb species or cultivars of species that are suitable for growing in your climate zone is crucial. (A cultivar is a variety of a species that has been created by humans. The word is short for *culti*vated *var*iety.) Many herbs that can be grown by short-season gardeners have numerous relatives that can't. Garden sage is a good case in point. This flavorful herb is just one of the over 900 species in the genus of plants known as *Salvia*, many of which make equally tasty culinary herbs. But while garden sage is winter hardy up to zone 4, most of the other sages are more tender, and must be cultivated indoors in pots, or as annuals. (Fragrant pineapple sage makes a lovely houseplant, or it can be grown as an annual.) Many heat-loving plants, including a number of species of *Salvia*, however, are just not suitable for growing in northern zones.

Understanding Soil pH Levels

The pH scale is used to measure soil characteristics. On a scale from 0 to 14, the lower the pH rating, the more acidic the soil; the higher the pH rating, the higher the soil's alkaline content. The middle of the pH scale, 7.0, is considered neutral. Highly acidic soils are too sour for most plants, while plants growing in highly alkaline soils usually produce poorly. If you garden in a high rainfall area, your soil is likely to be highly acidic. Conversely, if you garden in a dry area, your soil probably has a high alkaline content. Many culinary herbs are native to the Mediterranean area, a region of limestone soils, and so do best in near-neutral soils. Generally speaking, a good garden soil is slightly acidic, with a pH of 6.5. (Do-it-yourself pH testing kits are available from garden suppliers and mail-order nurseries.) Since different herbs do best within certain pH ranges, we have given the recommended or tolerated pH range for each of the herbs profiled in the "Culinary Herb Compendium." You can amend or improve highly acidic soils by adding lime. Soils with a high alkaline content benefit from the addition of sphagnum (peat moss).

While some gardeners thrive on the challenge of attempting to cultivate truly tender herb species and cultivars in our less than hospitable northern climate zones, we believe that our short growing season is enough of a handicap for most plants. And you needn't feel cheated, as there are suitable cultivars available for many culinary herbs, including such kitchen standbys as basil, oregano, parsley, garden sage, and thyme.

Container Herbs

Many herbs can be grown in containers, which may be either sunk directly in the ground when there is no further risk of frost, or placed on sunny porches or decks, where they may impart their beauty and fragrance to otherwise uninspired settings. (And if you place the pots as close to your kitchen door as possible, you'll find it convenient for spur-of-the-moment picking.) Once summer is over, just bring your container herbs back inside. Containers are ideal for marginally cold-tolerant herbs like rosemary, and essential for warm-season varieties like lemon verbena, ginger, and lemon grass (see "Warm-Season Container Herbs to Overwinter Indoors," which begins on page 170). Generally, you won't need more than a pot of each variety to satisfy the average family's requirements.

Start Seedlings Indoors

The surest way to get a head start on the growing season is to sow seeds indoors so that you'll have seedlings ready to plant outdoors as soon as the warmer weather arrives. (You'll find complete instructions in "Growing and Caring for Your Herbs," starting on page 17.) There are other advantages to raising your own seedlings: seeds are cheaper than buying bedding plants; growing plants from seeds is one of the most rewarding and enjoyable pastimes available to any gardener; and there is greater variety available in seeds than there is in purchased bedding plants.

Not all herbs are propagated from seeds, however. Herbs such as Greek oregano, the mints, and English lavender don't reproduce reliably from seeds, so you're better off buying plants. Garlic grows from cloves, and horseradish is propagated from root cuttings taken from an existing plant. (The propagation requirements for all the herbs in the "Culinary Herb Compendium" are given in the "Cultivation Notes.")

From a garden management perspective, herb seeds are of 2 kinds: those that can be started indoors with the seedlings being transplanted to the garden in the spring when the danger of frost is past, and those that should be sown outdoors where the plants are to grow. Lemon balm, basil, and sweet marjoram, for example, can be started indoors. Herbs that should be started outdoors include fenugreek, chervil, and the chamomiles. Some herb species require out-door planting because they produce seedlings with roots that do not take kindly to being trans-planted.

Before you place your seed order with a catalog supplier or dash off to your local nursery, seed list in hand, divide your selection into so-called indoor and outdoor seeds. Now consider care-fully the size of your indoor group and the growing conditions available in your home. Are you able to provide all the light, space, and attention required for the seeds to germinate and grow? As cheering as it is to see trays of seedlings growing on a windowsill, once you've taken inven-tory of your available windowsills with a desired sunny southern exposure, you may decide to cut back on your indoor seed order, purchasing a mixture of plants and seeds instead. There is no shame attached to buying nursery plants; the whole point of the exercise it to get the most out of the short outdoor growing season that we all have to work with.

While experienced gardeners usually opt for starting seeds indoors wherever possible, if you're new to growing herbs, you may wish to start your indoor seeding efforts with just a couple of varieties, and rely on buying nursery plants to get your herb garden under way.

Use Season Extenders

If time and temperature are not the natural allies of cold-climate gardeners, season extenders are. Season extenders, which range from the pricey greenhouse to the inexpensive row cover, can be used at both ends of the growing season. All serve the same purpose, which is to allow you the longest growing season possible for your herbs.

Whether you have a glass greenhouse attached to your home or whether you use a freestanding plastic floating row cover, the principle is the same, that is, the sun's rays shine into your growing area and do not easily pass out through the glass or the plastic. As a result, the sun's warmth is absorbed by everything inside the growing area. Ventilation is crucial in all season extenders because the trapped heat can cause the temperature inside the structure to rise dramatically, with disastrous consequences for the plants. This problem is particularly acute on an unseasonably, and unexpectedly, warm spring day.

Greenhouses

An attached greenhouse with a southern exposure, like the one shown on page 9, is ideal for starting seedlings. Such greenhouses are not inexpensive, and you may require a building permit in order to construct one. An attached greenhouse is usually designed to provide standing room for the gardener. It includes many shelves on which to place germinating seeds, growing seedlings, and at the end of the growing season, those herbs which need to winter indoors in containers.

The window greenhouse, a simple, much cheaper variation on the attached greenhouse, is built on the outside of any sunny window. While a window greenhouse will only give you an arm's-length cultivating area, this will still be more space than is available on the average windowsill. Both window greenhouses and attached greenhouses enable you to monitor your plants closely from the comfortable warmth of your home.

You can make a detached greenhouse quite inexpensively and easily by attaching plastic film to a simple A-frame wooden construction. Make the frame tall enough to allow you to stand inside, and line the interior with wooden shelves that can be supported by bricks or milk crates—whatever you have at hand. The downside of a detached greenhouse is that it is unheated, which means you can only use it in the spring after the danger of deep freezes is past.

A cold frame enables you to start your plants early in the season. Like greenhouses, cold frames trap heat. Hinged windows that you can prop open make it easy to provide ventilation and prevent overheating.

Cold Frames

A cold frame is a miniature unheated greenhouse. Cold frames are either permanent or temporary structures. While a permanent cold frame has solid walls made of wood, the walls of a temporary cold frame can be constructed of any reasonably lightweight material such as bales of straw. Whether permanent or temporary, the walls of the cold frame rest directly on the ground (a wooden floor is unnecessary). The top is covered with clear plastic or glass, which is often mounted in a hinged frame to provide ventilation as needed. Although you can make your solid cold frame whatever size you want, small is best, because then you can move the frame easily to different areas of the garden as required. Certainly, a cold frame 1 m x 2 m (3 feet x 6 feet) is big enough to hold sufficient seedlings to meet the herb needs of most families.

The best location for a cold frame is a sheltered spot with a southern exposure. When constructing your frame, make the back north-facing side about 15 cm (6 inches) higher than the south-facing lower front wall. The reason for the tilt is simple. The farther north you live, the lower the sun hangs in the southern sky early and late in the growing season. A cold frame with a tilted cover allows for the maximum amount of sunshine to reach your plants. It also permits the rain to run off. The usual size for cold frame boxes is 30 cm (12 inches) high in front and 45 cm (18 inches) in the back.

As cold frames are not artificially heated, be prepared to protect your plants on a very cold night by covering your frame with an old blanket. Conversely, you must provide ventilation on mild and sunny days to prevent overheating. Lifting the top to one side is usually all that's required.

Hot Beds

A hot bed is a cold frame that has a source of heat. The time-honored method employs fresh manure as the heat source. Dig a pit about 0.6 m (2 feet) where you wish to locate your cold frame. Pack the pit with fresh manure to around 20 cm (8 inches) from the surface of the pit. Fill the rest of the pit with topsoil. As the manure decomposes, it warms the soil.

If you garden in the city, working with fresh manure is not feasible. As an alternative, you can make a hot bed by using a waterproof electric cable, with a thermostat set at 18°C (65°F). (You can buy waterproof electric cables from a hardware store or an electrical supply company. Some nurseries also stock them.) The cable, which needs to be enclosed in a frame 35 cm (14 inches) deep in front and 48 cm (19 inches) deep in the back, should be buried 15 cm (6 inches) in the ground. Although the thermostat takes the guesswork out of raising your seedlings, electrically heated hot beds do dry out, so check your plants daily and water as required.

Floating Row Covers, Cloches, and Water Jackets

These temporary structures are designed to protect plants until the danger of frost is past. Floating row covers, which are typically made out of thin, transparent spun polyester or polyethylene supported by metal hoops, are light enough to be placed directly on newly seeded or planted areas. They warm up the soil and so speed up the maturation process of the plants. The covers are often slitted to vent heat on sunny days and may be made of fabrics that permit water to come through. If you use a double layer of plastic, row covers will also provide frost protection down to −3°C (about 27°F). Cover the row cover with a blanket if you're expecting temperatures below this. Row covers made of fabrics such as Reemay have the added benefit of keeping insects off the young plants while still admitting light and promoting warmth. Remove the row cover when the plants are too big and/or all danger of frost is past.

There are several types of floating row covers, but all of them, including the one shown here, keep plants warm in the spring.

Cloches are transparent, dome-shaped covers that act as mini greenhouses, providing internal heat that allows seeds to germinate early and seedlings to develop more rapidly than in the outside cold air. Like all other plant protectors, cloches need to be monitored on sunny days, and even on partly sunny days, to make sure the plants underneath are not getting overheated. The illustration on page 16 shows a typical glass cloche, modeled on the classic French market gardener's protective bell-shaped jar. (*Cloche* is French for "bell.") You can buy a variety of cloches from nurseries and garden centers, or you can make your own easily from clear plastic jars or bottles. (If you're using large pop bottles, cut them in half to fit.) Wide-necked tall glass jars also work well.

Polyethylene water jackets, also known as "wall o'water" or water walls, act like a double-walled cloche with the added advantage of having water between the 2 walls. During the day, the sun heats the water, providing the plant with warmth. These mini solar heat systems provide a microclimate for the plant that can protect it from freezing should the temperature drop dramatically. Water jackets are usually available from nurseries and garden centers.

Cloches provide individual plants with warmth and some protection from the cold. Traditional glass cloches like this one are expensive, but much cheaper plastic models are available. On hot spring days, a cloche must be ventilated or the plant inside could be badly overheated. To ventilate, just prop up one side, as shown here.

Warm the Soil with Plastic Film

You can warm the soil in your garden bed in advance of planting either seeds or seedlings by covering your growing area with clear or black plastic film. Although clear plastic is better for warming, black plastic has the added advantage of controlling weeds. Both work well as moisture retainers.

Before covering your well-tilled growing area with plastic, water the ground thoroughly. Spread the plastic over your bed, anchoring it at the edges with soil or stones, and in the middle with some strategically placed stones. When you're ready to plant, slash X's in the plastic where you intend to put your seedlings. If you're sowing seeds directly in the garden, cut a slit in the plastic to accommodate your seed row. You can also lift up the plastic and plant your seeds, but remember to slash the plastic as soon as the seedlings appear or they will expire. If you want to get more than one season's use out of your plastic, make sure that what you buy is at least 0.1 mm (4 mil) thick.

A water jacket is like a hot water bottle for plants. A garden hose is used to fill the space between the double walls of the translucent plastic "jacket" with water. The water retains the sun's heat very well, providing the plant with warmth at night.

GROWING AND CARING FOR YOUR HERBS

Herb seed catalogs usually come out at the beginning of January. Depending on when you place your order, you can expect your seeds to arrive in the mail sometime from January to the end of March. Alternatively, you can buy seeds from your local nursery. (Unless your herb garden is large, or you plan on using a particular herb extensively as a border plant—bergamot is a delightfully fragrant example—just purchase a single packet of seeds of each herb you plan on starting indoors.) Once you have your seeds, divide them into those that need to be started indoors and those that must be planted outdoors.

Seeding Indoors
Indoor seeding usually begins at the end of February or in early March. As the germination period and growth rate of seeds varies, you'll need to start your indoor herbs at different times. Winter savory, for example, should be started 10 weeks before you expect to be able to plant the seedlings outdoors. Lemon balm and garden thyme can be started indoors 8 to10 weeks before transplanting. Allow 8 weeks for bergamot, 6 to 8 weeks for sweet marjoram and catnip, 6 weeks for basil, 4 to 6 weeks for parsley, and 4 weeks for nasturtium. (You'll find indoor seeding times included in the "Compendium of Culinary Herbs.")

Last Spring Frost Date
Another important factor in the when-to-start-seeds-indoors calculation is the date when there is a 90 percent probability of not having a spring frost, 0°C (32°F), in your gardening location. Once you know this date, popularly known as the last spring frost date, you can work backwards from it to determine when to start planting indoors. For example, if you're gardening in Portland, Maine, your estimated last spring frost date is May 10. To have basil seedlings ready to plant outdoors when there is only a 10 percent danger of frost, subtract 6 weeks from this date. This simple arithmetic tells you that you should start basil indoors around March 29. If you're gardening in St. John's, Newfoundland, your last spring frost date is not until June 12, so you should hold off starting your basil indoors until around May 1.

To find out the estimated last spring frost date for your area, check with your local nursery, horticultural society, county extension agent, or department of agriculture. Web sites with information for many cities can also be found. And ask your experienced gardening neighbors. Keep in mind that there is a 10 percent risk of frost after your last spring frost date.

Examples of Estimated Dates of Last Spring Frost

Province/State	City	Frost Date
Alberta	Calgary	May 28
Alberta	Edmonton	May 15
British Columbia	Kamloops	May 2
British Columbia	Vancouver	March 31
British Columbia	Victoria	April 13
Colorado	Denver	May 3
Maine	Portland	May 10
Manitoba	Winnipeg	May 25
Montana	Helena	June 23
New Brunswick	Fredericton	May 18
New Hampshire	Concord	May 11
New York	Albany	April 27
New York	Canton	May 9
Newfoundland	St. John's	June 12
North Dakota	Bismark	May 11
Northwest Territories	Yellowknife	May 30
Nova Scotia	Halifax	May 15
Ontario	Ottawa	May 15
Ontario	Thunder Bay	May 31
Ontario	Toronto	April 20
Pennsylvania	Altoona	May 6
Pennsylvania	Pittsburgh	April 20
Pennsylvania	Scranton	April 24
Prince Edward Island	Charlottetown	May 16
Quebec	Gaspé	May 26
Quebec	Montréal	May 5
Quebec	Sherbrooke	May 12
Saskatchewan	Saskatoon	May 27
South Dakota	Huron	May 4
Vermont	Burlington	May 8
Washington	Seattle	March 14
Washington	Yakima	April 15
Wisconsin	Green Bay	May 6
Wisconsin	Milwaukee	April 20
Wyoming	Cheyenne	May 14
Yukon Territory	Whitehorse	June 5

Seeding Containers

Once you've determined your indoor planting schedule, it's time to make sure you have an adequate supply of suitable seeding containers. While you can buy seeding containers from nurseries and garden centers, you can make perfectly adequate receptacles from recycled milk cartons, margarine and dairy tubs, and plastic, paper, or polystyrene drink cups. Your homemade containers should be about 8 cm (3 inches) deep, so don't use egg cartons as the indentations are too small. The 4- or 6-pack small pots that nursery plants are often sold in make ideal seeding containers, so plan on keeping these from now on, if you have been in the habit of discarding them. You can also use an open flat or tray to start your seeds, although you'll need to take extra care not to damage the entangled roots when you transplant the seedlings to larger pots. To prevent disease, all recycled containers must be thoroughly washed in hot soapy water. Make drainage holes in the bottom of each container.

You can also start your seeds in soil blocks, or in peat pellets, which are plugs of compressed peat moss mixed with plant nutrients and enclosed in plastic netting. Soak the pellet in water and it swells into a mini pot in which to sow your seeds. You may also want to invest in one of those handy gadgets that enable you to form pots from old newspaper. Biodegradable containers such as these can be planted directly in the garden when it's time to move the seedlings outdoors, thereby minimizing root damage to young plants.

Joined fiber pots, peat blocks, and recycled food vessels all make good containers for seedlings.

Soil for Your Seeds and Seedlings

Give your seedlings a head start by preparing a good starting medium for the seeds. A reliable mix consists of equal parts of loam, garden sand, and compost or peat moss. Because seedlings are susceptible to damping-off, a fungus disease found in the soil, you'll need to sterilize your starting medium before you plant your seeds, or run the risk of having your seedlings expire shortly after they appear. Sterilize soil by baking it in the oven for an hour at 85°C (185°F). Alternatively, put the soil in a bucket and pour boiling water over it, stirring the soil mix as you pour. Let the mix cool. and strain it before using. Sterilized potting soil mixtures from garden centers can also be used.

Young seedlings develop strong root systems quickly in soil that is light and porous. Mixing vermiculite in your soil will lighten it, and because it's a sterile medium, vermiculite will not introduce disease into the mix. Vermiculite, which is available at your nursery or garden center, is a mica compound that both holds water well and contains some nutrients. The added advantage of a light soil is that it makes it easier to transplant the seedlings without damaging their roots.

Because a seed contains enough nutrients to meet the young plant's needs until its true leaves form, you can also start seeds in vermiculite or perlite, another sterile medium. The first leaves that the plant produces, called seedling leaves or cotyledons, lack the serrated edges and/or other features that often characterize the true leaves of many plants. Once the true leaves form, however, you must transplant the seedlings to your soil mix.

Sowing Your Seeds

Before filling your containers with the prepared soil mix, you need to moisten it. Put the soil in a plastic bag, add water, stir, and close the bag. Then let it sit for a couple of hours to let the soil absorb the water. You don't want mud, so go easy on the amount of water to start off with. When the time is up, open the bag, put some soil in the palm of your hand and squeeze it. If the soil crumbles when you open your hand, your mix is damp enough to use. Fill your containers with the prepared soil mix to within 6 mm (¼ inch) of the top. Press the soil down lightly. If you are starting seeds in a sterile medium (vermiculite or perlite), fill the containers as above, and water lightly with tepid water.

Check the seed packets or the "Cultivation Notes" in the "Culinary Herb Compendium" for the planting depth for individual herbs. As a general rule of thumb, seeds sown in containers should be planted to a depth of about 1 to 3 times their diameter. (Deeper levels are often recommended for outdoor plantings because the soil dries faster.) Press seeds down gently and cover sparingly with soil mix. Very small seeds like those of anise hyssop should just be lightly pressed into the surface of the soil. Spray the surface with water. Continue to keep the soil damp, but do not overwater as soggy soil can lead to damping-off. Seeds planted in vermiculite or perlite are planted in the same fashion and are then covered with the sterile medium and sprayed lightly. Again, avoid overwatering, but don't let the medium dry out. Be sure to label each seed container with the name of the herb that you've planted.

Lighting Needs

Cover your containers with plastic wrap or put each container in a plastic bag, and then put the containers in a warm, dark place. Check that excessive condensation isn't occurring, as the humidity encourages molds. If there are hanging drops of water on the plastic, put some holes in it. Alternatively, you can put the seed containers on a sunny windowsill, but without their plastic coverings. (Some seeds germinate better in the light, so check seed packages for specific lighting requirements.) Germination times vary according to seed variety: anise hyssop seedlings may emerge as soon as 4 days after planting, lemon balm and basil seedlings take at least 8 days to put in an appearance, while garden thyme seedlings don't appear until 2 weeks after planting.

An indoor fluorescent light stand meets the lighting needs of growing seedlings, without the risk of overheating the young plants.

Seeds set to germinate under plastic wrap or in plastic bag "greenhouses" must be liberated from their plastic coverings as soon as the seedlings emerge. Growing seedlings need to be exposed to bright light otherwise their stems will be long and spindly. Such unhealthy plants will not do well when transplanted outdoors. Put the seedlings on a sunny windowsill. You'll need a southern or southwestern exposure to provide adequate light, assuming of course that the days are always sunny. As this assumption hardly ever holds up in our northern climate, you must compensate for the lack of sunshine by providing artificial light. (Besides, the average home only has so many south-facing windowsills!)

Fluorescent light is best, because it is bright but not hot like household incandescent bulbs, and so will not overheat your seedlings. You can purchase and install commercial grow-light fluorescents, which come with instructions for use. A couple of 40-watt fluorescent tubes, one cool white, the other warm, will also work, providing light to an area about 1.2 m x 1.8 m (4 feet x 6 feet). Your light source should be no more than 15 cm (6 inches) from the tops of the growing seedlings, otherwise they will become spindly as they stretch for the light. Bear in mind that the best lighting from the tubes will be in the middle, so you'll have to move the containers around to ensure maximum lighting for all the seedlings. Newly emerged seedlings can usually be given continuous light for the first 2 weeks. After that, about 16 hours a day is sufficient. Leave the lights off at night to give the plants a rest. To prevent the plants from growing crookedly, give the containers a quarter-turn each morning.

If you're raising seedlings on a windowsill, be prepared to move them at night if the thermometer drops. Tender seedlings will suffer if left to spend the night on a chilly windowsill. Return the seedlings to the windowsill in the morning.

Watering and Thinning

In addition to light, seedlings need moisture. Check the seedlings once a day to see if they need to be watered. If the seedlings are beginning to wilt, you'll know it's time to water again. You can also press the soil at the top of the container to see if it's drying out. The press test is not reliable if you're using vermiculite (or perlite), as the surface of the vermiculite can feel quite dry, even while there is sufficient moisture down at the root level. Seedlings prefer tepid water rather than cold tap water, and you should stop watering when you see water coming out of the drainage holes at the bottom of the container.

If your containers are overcrowded, you'll need to thin the seedlings. Thinning is essential for healthy, vigorous plants with stocky stems. Use a pair of tweezers to remove the unwanted seedlings, or cut them at the soil's surface with a small pair of scissors. Thin carefully, as you don't want to disturb the roots of the remaining plants. Leave about 6 mm (¼ inch) space between the remaining seedlings.

Transplanting Indoors

Once your seedlings have their true leaves, they will need to be transplanted into individual containers. If you're using recycled containers, wash them thoroughly in hot soapy water. Provide drainage holes at the bottom, and fill with soil mix. Water your seedlings before transplanting them. Then use a table fork to loosen the seedlings carefully. Lift the seedlings gently out of their original container. Poke a hole large enough to accommodate a seedling's roots in the soil mix in your new container. Holding the plant by its seedling leaves (cotyledons), plant it in the hole, and press the soil around it. Water lightly. Fertilize the plants once a week with a dilute solution of fish emulsion, or a balanced liquid fertilizer.

Hardening Off

Before you transplant your seedlings outdoors, they need to be hardened off or readied gradually for the relatively harsher conditions of their permanent location in the herb garden. About 10 days before your outdoor transplanting date—and providing the day is warm and not windy—put the plants outside in a shady spot and leave them there for about an hour. Then bring them inside. Repeat the process the next day, only leave them out in the shade for 2 hours. On the third day, give them an hour in the sun in addition to a couple of hours in the shade. As the days unfold, increase the plants' exposure to the sun. By the end of the hardening-off period, your plants should be able to stay outdoors all day and all night as well, as long as there is no danger of frost. Cut back on watering during the hardening-off stage. You don't want the soil to be constantly moist, just moist enough so that the plants don't wilt. Plants can also be hardened off in a cold frame.

Transplanting Outdoors

Ready your planting location for your herb seedlings by removing any weeds and stones. (If you've been warming your soil with plastic film, you'll need to roll it up temporarily.) Rake the soil well, ensuring that there are no clods and that the texture is friable or crumbly. Finally, water the bed, making sure it's thoroughly damp, but not muddy. (Don't forget to re-lay the plastic film.)

Transplant your seedlings on a calm, cloudy day. Make sure the hole you dig for each seedling is bigger than its root system. After you place each plant in its hole, fill in the hole with soil, taking care to press the soil down firmly around the plant's stem.

If you raised your seedlings in peat pots, carefully cut away the bottom of each pot to give the roots more room, then transplant the entire potted plant, including the pot. If you used peat pellets with a net covering, slash the netting on each side before you put the pellet in the soil.

Now is the time to help your seedlings reach maturity quicker by providing them with season extenders such as a portable cold frame, floating row covers, cloches, and water jackets.

Seeding Outdoors

Sow seeds directly in the garden on a bright sunny day. Use a stick or trowel to make furrows in the soil in which to plant your seeds, following the depth directions given in the "Cultivation Notes" in the "Compendium of Culinary Herbs." Fine seeds, like those of Oriental poppy, are just scattered on the surface of the soil. Identify your seed rows with wooden or plastic plant markers. Water, using a fine spray. Extra protection can be provided by placing your portable cold frame over the seeded area, or covering with a floating row cover.

Like indoor seedlings, outdoor seedlings also require thinning. For healthy growth, the developing plants should be far enough apart so that they do not touch each other. For especially sensitive plants, cover individual seedlings with a cloche or water jacket.

Preparing for Winter

All too soon summer starts to wind down. As the days grow shorter and the temperature starts to drop, the risk of an early frost becomes real. Now is the time to act to make the most of what's left of the season and to ready your herb garden for winter.

Examples of Estimated Dates of First Fall Frost

Province/State	City	Frost Date
Alberta	Calgary	September 15
Alberta	Edmonton	September 23
British Columbia	Kamloops	October 5
British Columbia	Vancouver	November 5
British Columbia	Victoria	November 5
Colorado	Denver	September 20
Maine	Portland	September 18
Manitoba	Winnipeg	September 22
Montana	Helena	August 25
New Brunswick	Fredericton	September 22
New Hampshire	Concord	September 30
New York	Albany	October 13
New York	Canton	September 26
Newfoundland	St. John's	October 12
North Dakota	Bismark	September 24
Northwest Territories	Yellowknife	September 15
Nova Scotia	Halifax	October 20
Ontario	Ottawa	October 5
Ontario	Thunder Bay	September 15
Ontario	Toronto	October 6
Pennsylvania	Altoona	October 4
Pennsylvania	Pittsburgh	October 23
Pennsylvania	Scranton	October 14
Prince Edward Island	Charlottetown	October 9
Quebec	Gaspé	September 30
Quebec	Montréal	October 7
Quebec	Sherbrooke	September 10
Saskatchewan	Saskatoon	September 19
South Dakota	Huron	September 30
Vermont	Burlington	October 3
Washington	Seattle	November 24
Washington	Yakima	October 22
Wisconsin	Green Bay	October 13
Wisconsin	Milwaukee	October 25
Wyoming	Cheyenne	October 2
Yukon Territory	Whitehorse	August 25

First Fall Frost Date

An early fall frost, even if followed by the balmier temperatures of an Indian summer, spells the end of your tender herbs, and the end of the growing process for perennial herbs that overwinter outdoors. "First fall frost dates" are calculated as the dates in a region before which there is only a 10 percent probability of freezing temperatures, so 90 percent of the time your garden plants will survive longer than the fall first frost date. Knowing the estimated date of the first fall frost in your growing area will help you plan your strategy for prolonging the outdoor season of your annuals. You also need to err on the side of caution in planning on bringing container herbs back into the house for the winter. Working back from this date enables you to give your perennials a head start on enduring the coming winter. Of course, as first fall frost dates are not fixed, you'll need to pay attention to weather forecasts and the advice of seasoned gardening neighbors.

Providing Frost Protection

If frost is expected, cover your annuals in the late afternoon with floating row covers. Putting old blankets over the row covers will provide extra protection, and added warmth. For those plants that are too tall for a row cover, fashion makeshift protection out of old sheets, blankets, garbage bags, or sheets of plastic. Anything that keeps the frost from the plants will do, just be sure to anchor your covering so that it does not blow off during the night.

If a light frost catches you unprepared, you can head off the potential damage by lightly watering the plants. Because water releases heat as it freezes, timing is crucial. The plants must be watered before the sun reaches them.

While covering annuals will protect them from light to moderate frosts, there is not much you can do when a heavy frost strikes.

Mulching and Wrapping Perennials for Winter Survival

About a month before your estimated first fall frost date, stop harvesting your perennial herbs to discourage the plants from putting out tender, new growth. Mulch perennial herbs after the first frost to help them survive the winter. Straw makes the best mulch as it doesn't pack down and smother the plants. If straw is not available, you can also use well-rotted manure, leaves, or peat moss. Mulch each plant to a depth of 10 to 15 cm (4 to 6 inches).

Don't cut the foliage back to the ground in the fall, but leave some of the withered branches to trap and hold the snow, which will protect the plant's crown from alternating freezing and thawing. While heavy snow coverage is one of the best protectors against cold and drying winds, nature does not always oblige. In addition to mulching, wrap your shrubby herbs in burlap to provide extra protection. Refer to the "Cultivation Notes" in the "Compendium of Culinary Herbs" for specific overwintering requirements.

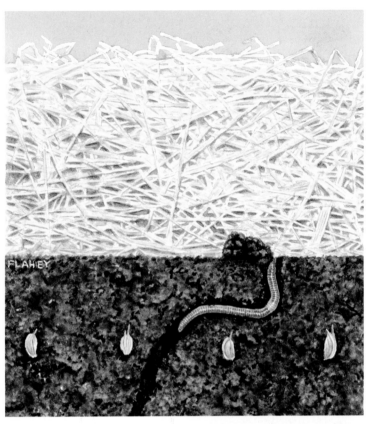

Garlic cloves planted in the fall need to be well mulched to survive the winter. Although the cloves may sprout in the fall, the straw will protect the short shoots. In the spring, just leave the straw and the shoots will grow through and above it. The mulch also prevents weed seeds from producing weeds.

Help your perennials to overwinter outdoors successfully by mulching died-down herbaceous plants and wrapping shrubby varieties in burlap.

CULINARY HERB COMPENDIUM

Chives

Lemon marigold (Tagetes tenuifolia), *cultivar Orange has very tasty flowers.*

Lemon marigold (Tagetes tenuifolia), *cultivar Lemon Gem has equally delectable blooms.*

28

AGRIMONY *Agrimonia eupatoria*
Rosaceae (rose family)
Also known as: Church steeples, cockle-bur, harvest lice, liverwort, rat's tail, stickwort, white tansy

Zone
3
Coldest
Tolerated

DESCRIPTION
- Agrimony, which is found in most of Europe, northern Africa, Asia Minor, and in northern and central Asia, is a pleasantly aromatic, hardy perennial that also makes an attractive garden ornamental or shady border plant. It grows from 30 to 150 cm (1 to 5 feet) tall.
- Serrated, compound leaves arise from a green stem, and vary in length from about 25 cm (10 inches) to less than 8 cm (3 inches) at the top. The bottom leaves alternate pairs of small and large leaflets. The leaves have a sweetish, apricot-like fragrance.
- Woody rootstock is branched and spreading.
- Long, pointed stalks produce numerous small, honey-flavored, yellow flowers that are reminiscent of church spires. Agrimony blooms from June to September.
- Fruit is enclosed in a top-shaped, hardened case with spreading hooked bristles around the middle. These bristles easily catch onto passing fur, feathers, or the clothes of passersby, promoting wide seed dispersal.
- Flowers, leaves, and stems are all edible.

CULTIVATION NOTES
- Agrimony grows in most types of soil. It is naturally adapted to alkaline soils, but also tolerates somewhat acidic soil. While easy to cultivate in dry soil, the plants do need water during dry periods or they may not flower.
- Prefers full sun, but keep the soil moderately moist. Also tolerates partial shade.
- Sow seeds outdoors in the early spring. (You can improve germination considerably by storing the seeds in damp soil in the refrigerator for 6 weeks prior to planting.) Plant seeds 1 cm (½ inch) deep. Once established, agrimony tends to self-seed.
- May also be propagated by root division. Divide the plants in spring to provide time for the winter buds to form. When dividing the crown, be sure to include a live stem.
- Space plants 25 cm (10 inches) apart.
- Usually pest- and disease-free.
- Overwinters outdoors up to zone 3.

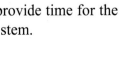

> *Agrimony comes from the Greek* αρgεμα, *meaning "a fleck in the eye," a term used by the ancient Greeks for those plants that were used for treating eye conditions.*
>
> *The term* eupatoria *is derived from Mithridates VI Eupator (132–63 BC), one of the kings of Pontus, who was a renowned herbalist.*

HARVESTING NOTES

- Pick the leaves, flowers, and stems in early summer, when the plant is in flower. All parts may be used fresh or dried.
- To dry agrimony, spread out the leaves, flowers, and stems on a wire rack in a warm, shaded location. When dry, crumble the material to powder, and store in airtight jars.

CULINARY USES

- For a pleasant honey-flavored tea, steep 5 to 10 mL (1 to 2 teaspoons) of powdered agrimony or 15 mL (3 teaspoons) of lightly crushed fresh agrimony in 250 mL (1cup) of boiling water. If desired, sweeten with honey or flavor with licorice.
- Add the flowers to home-brewed beer.

CRAFT USES

- Include fragrant agrimony in sweet-smelling sachets and potpourris.

MEDICINAL USES

- In herbal folk medicine, agrimony was used to treat a variety of ailments. The astringent quality of the tannins in agrimony made it a traditional remedy for treating diarrhea. It is still employed in some European commercial herbal medicinal teas used to treat liver and bile problems.
- Agrimony tea has a deserved reputation for promoting urination. Medical research suggests that agrimony may well be useful for treating some gastrointestinal disorders.
- Tannins cause flesh to contract, so agrimony, with its high tannin content, has been used for centuries as a home remedy for minor bleeding. Studies indicate that agrimony may have legitimate medicinal value for treating some skin conditions.
- Agrimony contains vitamins B_1, K, and ascorbic acid (vitamin C).

CAUTIONS

- Agrimony may cause some people to experience photodermatitis, a skin rash that appears after eating the herb and subsequently being exposed to sunlight.

- Some studies have shown that agrimony can lower blood pressure. Don't consume this herb if you are undergoing anticoagulant therapy or drug treatment for high or low blood pressure.
- Agrimony is reputed to affect the menstrual cycle, so you should avoid it if you are pregnant or nursing.
- Because agrimony tea has a high tannin content, it should be consumed in moderation. Adding milk to your tea helps prevent tannins from being harmful.

> *In the Middle Ages, agrimony's common name "liverwort" came about because it was thought that the yellow flowers resembled the tint of an individual's skin during an attack of jaundice, and so the plant was believed to cure liver complaints.*

CULTIVARS AND RELATIVES

- 'Sweet Scented' agrimony. This cultivar is very popular in France for making tea. The leaves do indeed have a sweetish scent, while the flowers have an apricot-like fragrance, with a hint of spice.

ANGELICA *Angelica archangelica*
Umbelliferae (Apiaceae; carrot family)
Also known as: Archangel, European angelica, garden angelica, Holy Ghost plant, wild parsnip

Zone 4
Coldest Tolerated

DESCRIPTION

- Angelica, a vigorous herbaceous biennial or short-lived perennial native from northern and eastern Europe through central and east Asia and the Aleutian Islands, grows 2 to 3 m (6½ to 10 feet) high. Given its size, sweetly fragrant angelica makes a handsome focus for the back of your herb garden.
- Large, pointed, light green, compound leaves have serrated edges, and grow from sheaths surrounding the stem. The lower leaves can be as much as 0.6 to 1 m (2 to 3 feet) long.
- Angelica has a long, hollow, grooved, round stem, and long, thick, fleshy, spindle-shaped, reddish-brown roots.
- Tiny, honey-scented, greenish-white flowers bloom in umbrella-like clusters, about 15 cm (6 inches) across, and have a delicate, sweet-ish fragrance. Flowers bloom from June to August in the second or third year of the plant's growth.
- When the yellowish, oblong-shaped fruit ripens, it splits into a pair of winged seed cases.
- All parts of the plant—stem, leaves, seeds, and roots—are edible, and have a juniper-like flavor with a mildly spicy aftertaste.

CULTIVATION NOTES

- Angelica is naturally adapted to wet areas, so keep the soil moist throughout the growing season. Slightly acidic soil is best. Recommended pH range is 4.5 to 7.0.
- Prefers light shade, but will grow in sun, providing the ground is well mulched.
- Plant seeds outdoors as soon as the ground can be worked in the spring. Seeds must be fresh in order to germinate. As angelica does not transplant well, sow the seeds where you want the plants to grow.

- Purchased seeds may require refrigeration for 4 to 5 weeks prior to planting. (Reputable seed suppliers should have stored their seeds under refrigeration.) Seeds sown in the fall will receive the necessary cold treatment during the winter.
- Seeds need exposure to sunlight to germinate, so cover with a very fine layer of soil.
- Angelica can also be propagated from root cuttings, but plants grown from seeds are considered superior.
- Space plants 0.6 to 1 m (2 to 3 feet) apart.
- Flower stalks usually develop in the late spring of the plant's second year. In cooler areas, where angelica grows slowly, it may not flower until the third or fourth year.
- Plant usually dies after it has flowered and seeded, but if you remove the flowering stalks before the plant seeds, it may survive for another couple of growing seasons.
- Plants left to go to seed may self-sow.
- Susceptible to crown rot, and to infestations of aphids, leaf miners, earwigs, and spider mites.
- Overwinters outdoors up to zone 4.

> *Legend has it that angelica is so named because it flowers on the feast day of Michael the Archangel, May 8, according to the old Julian calendar.*

HARVESTING NOTES
- Collect the young stems and tender leaves for fresh use or drying early in the second year of growth. Harvest before the plant flowers.
- When the seed heads are almost ripe, enclose them in small paper bags so they won't fall apart. Hang the leaves and the enclosed seed heads to air-dry, then store in airtight containers.
- Roots for eating are most tender in the first year of growth. Harvest roots in the fall.

> *In 1665, the year of London's Great Plague, King Charles II issued a prescription entitled The King's Majesty's Excellent Recipe for the Plague. The King's cure, which was taken twice daily by thousands of desperate Londoners, included angelica.*

CULINARY USES
- Steam the stems and serve them buttered, like asparagus. Chopped stems are ideal for flavoring roast pork.
- Add chopped leaves to rhubarb for sweetness. Leaves are also excellent in soups, salads, herb mixtures, and in bouillon for fish and shellfish.
- Candy the young stems and use for decorating cakes and desserts.
- Brew a refreshing tea by adding 5 mL (1 teaspoon) of dried angelica or 15 mL (3 teaspoons) of crushed fresh leaves to 250 mL (1 cup) of boiling water. Allow to steep. Add honey or lemon to taste.
- Angelica is used in many liqueurs or aperitifs, such as Chartreuse. The juniper-flavored seeds are sometimes substituted for real juniper berries in making gin.

CRAFT USES

- Include the attractive seed heads in floral arrangements.

MEDICINAL USES

- In traditional folk medicine, angelica was widely used in the past to treat a variety of illnesses, but it's not considered to be medically useful today.
- The essential oil from angelica is used commercially in the manufacture of perfume, soap, toothpaste, skin cream, and shampoo.
- Angelica is rich in vitamin C and potassium.

In medieval times, Carmelite water, which included crushed angelica roots, was widely drunk as a protection against witches' spells. Angelica was also believed to be the only herb witches did not use. As a result, having angelica in her garden or home was a good defense for a woman accused of witchcraft.

CAUTIONS

- Some people may experience dermatitis from handling angelica.
- As angelica contains potentially harmful chemicals called coumarins, it's best to consume it in moderation.
- The coumarins of angelica thin blood, so individuals on anticoagulant therapy should avoid this herb.
- Because angelica was once used in very large quantities as an abortifacient and is also reputed to affect the menstrual cycle, you should not consume it if you are pregnant or nursing.

Laplanders used to crown their poets with a wreath of angelica to inspire them, and it was customary for everyone to chew dry angelica root to promote longevity.

BALM, LEMON *Melissa officinalis*

Labiatae (Lamiaceae; mint family)

Also known as: Balm mint, common balm, English balm, garden balm, honey plant, sweet balm

Zone 4

Coldest Tolerated

DESCRIPTION

- Lemon balm is a delightfully fragrant, fairly hardy, bushy perennial that grows 20 to 75 cm (8 to 30 inches) tall. Cultivated as a culinary herb from antiquity, lemon balm was highly prized by the Greeks and Romans as a honeybee plant. It is a native of the eastern Mediterranean region southward to Israel and Syria, and eastward through the Crimea, the Caucasus, and northern Iran to Tien Shan and Pamir.
- Light green, veined leaves have serrated edges. Young leaves have a refreshing lemon flavor and scent.
- Lemon balm has an upright, branching stem, and thin, yellowish-brown roots and rhizomes (underground stems).
- Produces sparse clusters of small, white, or yellowish-white flowers in midsummer. Flowers bloom where the leaves join the stems.
- May be grown indoors for winter use.
- Lemon balm is an excellent honeybee plant.

CULTIVATION NOTES

- Lemon balm grows best in rich, moist, well-drained, slightly acidic to slightly alkaline soil. Tolerated pH range is 4.5 to 7.6.
- Prefers full sun, but will do well in partial shade.
- Plant seeds indoors, about 8 to 10 weeks before your last spring frost date. Seeds need light to germinate, so plant to a depth of no more than 6 mm (¼ inch). Seedlings emerge in 8 to 10 days. Transplant seedlings outdoors after danger of frost is passed.
- Space plants about 45 to 60 cm (18 to 24 inches) apart.
- Seeds can also be planted outdoors in late fall, to lie dormant through the winter and germinate in the following spring.
- Can also be propagated by stem cuttings and root division. Take stem cuttings from vigorous summer growth. Divide roots in spring or fall, ensuring that each divided section has 3 or 4 buds. If you divide roots in fall, plant divided sections early enough to allow them to become established. Mulch for winter protection.

- Encourage tender growth by dividing plants in spring or fall every 3 or 4 years.
- Pinch back tops to increase the foliage and to discourage flowers from developing.
- Weed regularly, but be careful not to injure the shallow roots.
- Once established, lemon balm self-sows freely and will spread if unchecked.
- Attacked by chewing and sucking insects, but generally pest-free. Susceptible to powdery mildew late in the season.
- Overwinters outdoors up to zone 4. In very cold areas, mulch the plants well to protect the roots.
- Plants grown indoors require at least 5 hours of direct sunlight or 14 to 16 hours of artificial light daily. Keep the plants pruned back to about 20 cm (8 inches), and harvest while young.

In ancient Greece, lemon balm leaves were used to treat scorpion stings and bites from venomous beasts.

HARVESTING NOTES

- For immediate use, harvest young leaves anytime during the growing season. Cut leaves early in the morning after the dew has evaporated. Handle the fresh leaves carefully as they bruise and become discolored easily.
- Leaves are at their best early in the year. As the leaves age, the fragrance deteriorates and they begin to taste stale and musty, so cut back the plants regularly to ground level to produce fresh shoots.
- To dry lemon balm, cut the plants back to ground level as the flowers begin to appear. Hang the harvested plants to dry in a shady, airy location. Once the leaves are crisply dry, store in airtight jars.
- Freeze leaves in ice cubes.

The Swiss alchemist and physician Paracelsus (1493–1541) called lemon balm "the elixir of life," and for centuries the plant was said to promote longevity.

CULINARY USES

- Add fresh or dried lemon balm leaves to salads, sandwiches, marinades, sauces, soups, stews, stuffing for pork, veal, or poultry, vegetables, egg dishes, jams, jellies, and herbal vinegar, in particular tarragon vinegar. As the taste of lemon balm is rather delicate, feel free to use it more generously than you would other more robust herbs.
- When using fresh leaves, crush them first to release the lemony flavor.
- Make a refreshing tea by pouring boiling water over a handful of fresh leaves. Steep for a few minutes. Sweeten with honey or sugar to taste.
- Add lemon balm to summer punches and soft drinks.
- Lemon balm oil is used as a flavoring in various liqueurs, including Chartreuse and Benedictine.

CRAFT USES
- Include fragrant lemon balm leaves in potpourris and sachets.

MEDICINAL USES
- Lemon balm oil is used in aromatherapy to help counter depression.
- Some studies have shown that lemon balm does act as a sedative.
- In Europe, lemon balm extracts are used in some non-prescription skin ointments.

CAUTIONS
- Individuals with a thyroid condition should exercise caution in consuming lemon balm, as it may interfere with the thyroid-stimulating hormone thyrotropin.
- Some people may experience dermatitis after excessive contact with lemon balm.
- Honeybees like lemon balm, so be careful there are none on the plants that you pick.

The genus name for lemon balm, Melissa, comes from the Greek word for "bee." Since antiquity, beekeepers have been advised to rub honeybee hives with lemon balm in order to attract new colonies. Curiously, while lemon balm oil is attractive to bees, it also acts as an insect repellant.

BASIL, SWEET *Ocimum basilicum*
Labiatae (Lamiaceae; mint family)
Also known as: Common basil, French basil, royal basil, royal herb

Annual

DESCRIPTION
- Basil, an essential culinary herb in every kitchen garden, is a tender annual that grows from 30 to 60 cm (12 to 24 inches) tall, with height varying according to cultivar. Basil's place of origin is unknown, but it's most likely native to tropical Africa.
- Leaf shape, color, flavor, and aroma vary according to cultivar. Sweet basil leaves are a glossy dark green with serrated or smooth edges. Leaves have a distinctive spicy-sweet, warm, clove-like aroma and flavor, with pungent undertones.
- Flowers of sweet basil are white, occasionally tinged with light purple. The tiny flowers, which are about 6 mm (¼ inch) long, are arranged in whorls on the flower stalk.
- May be grown as an indoor houseplant.

CULTIVATION NOTES
- Basil grows best in light, well-drained, nutrient-rich, slightly acidic soil. Tolerated pH range is 4.3 to 8.4.
- Requires full sun. Keep well watered, but avoid waterlogging.
- Plant seeds indoors, about 6 weeks before last spring frost date. Sow seeds 6 mm (¼ inch) deep. Keep soil moist until seeds germinate – about 8 to 14 days – but do not overwater. Prior to transplanting, trim tops of seedlings when they are about 15 cm (6 inches) tall, to encourage lateral branching and growth. Plant seedlings outdoors when all danger of frost is past.
- Space seedlings 30 to 45 cm (12 to 18 inches) apart.
- Does not tolerate temperatures below 5°C (41°F) well, so cover plants with a plastic row cover or cloches if the temperature dips.
- Pinch off the flower stalks so that the plants will continue to produce new leaves.
- Susceptible to leaf spot during periods of high humidity or if growing in poorly drained soil, and to infestations of aphids and thrips.
- If cultivating indoors as a winter kitchen plant, sow seeds shallowly in small, well-drained pots. Place pots in a warm, well-lit location. Transfer clumps of 3 to 5 plants to 10 cm

(4 inch) pots when the seedlings have the second pair of true leaves. Put pots in full sunlight. Plants need at least 5 hours of direct sunlight or 12 hours of artificial light daily. Don't overwater. Keep plants bushy by picking off young tips. Dwarf varieties such as 'Spicy Globe,' 'Minimum,' and 'Green Bouquet' are ideal for growing on a sunny windowsill.

Basil has a long history. It has been grown in Asia for over 3 000 years. The ancient Egyptians, Greeks, and Romans all cultivated basil. The name "basil" comes from the Greek basileus, *meaning "king," and indeed basil has often been called "the king of herbs."*

HARVESTING NOTES
- Harvest individual leaves at any time during the growing season. (The leaves are tastiest when the plants are young.)
- Use scissors or a sharp knife when harvesting just a few leaves, as clean cuts do the least damage to the plant.
- The entire upper stem and leaves can be harvested, but leave at least 4 sets of leaves – about 13 cm (5 inches) – or the plant may die. To ensure freshness, re-cut stems and put them in a jug of water in a cool location. Avoid wetting the leaves as they will become discolored.
- Blanch leaves and then freeze in ice cubes for later use. Freezing is the best way to preserve basil's flavor.
- To dry basil, strip the leaves from the stem and dry in a dark, airy location. Store dried leaves whole in an airtight container.

Basil is an important religious herb. Christians believe it may have grown on the grave of Jesus Christ. Saint Basil the Great (328–379), a saint of the Eastern Orthodox Church, is said to have discovered the Holy Cross with basil growing at its foot. To this day, Greek women take basil with them to church on Saint Basil's Day (January 1). In the Hindu and Islamic faiths, basil is planted on the graves of loved ones.

CULINARY USES
- Use fresh, frozen, or dried basil in soups, fish dishes, omelets, dressings, stuffing, pasta dishes, on pizza, and with vegetables such as artichoke, broccoli, carrots, eggplant, cabbage, squash, and zucchini. Basil is perhaps the best accompaniment to tomatoes, and is essential in tomato paste and tomato-based sauces and for making pesto, that delectable Italian sauce made from crushed basil leaves, garlic, olive oil, Parmesan cheese, and pine nuts.
- Add fresh leaves to salads.
- Small leaves should be used whole. Tear large leaves rather than cut them in order to preserve their flavor.
- When cooking with fresh basil, add the leaves towards the end of your recipe's cooking time for maximum flavor and aroma.
- Add fresh leaves to vinegar and virgin olive oil.

CRAFT USES
- Include sprigs of fragrant basil in fresh floral arrangements.

MEDICINAL USES
- Although widely used in the past for treating many ailments, and still used medicinally in many countries, sweet basil is basically a culinary herb.
- Basil is rich in vitamin C, potassium, beta-carotene, and calcium.

> *Boccaccio's Decameron, the well-known collection of Italian tales, includes a romantic story of a young woman who nurtured a basil plant using the corpse of her dead lover to fertilize it, even as she watered it with her tears.*

CULTIVARS AND RELATIVES
There are over 50 varieties of basil. Here's a selection for you to try:
- "Lettuce-leaved" cultivars. Available under many cultivar names, these basils have large leaves that are often crinkled. Look for 'Mammoth' – the flavorful, fragrant, all-purpose salad basil.
- "Lemon" cultivars. Not all cultivars with "lemon" in their name are true sweet basil. 'Mrs. Burns Lemon' is a reliable cultivar with a wonderful lemon scent and very pretty pink flowers.
- American basil (*O. americanum*) has produced several exceptional cultivars and hybrids. 'Genoa Profumatissima' or "perfume basil" has a floral scent and tastes intriguingly of citrus, anise, cinnamon, and mint. 'Dwarf Bouquet' is equally striking in scent and taste, but smaller in size. 'Sacred basil,' not to be confused with holy basil, has unusual clove-scented leaves. 'Green Ruffles,' which is a hybrid of American basil and sweet basil, has puckered leaves reminiscent of lettuce, and a very pleasant scent and taste. 'Spicy Globe,' another hybrid, has a pronounced spicy flavor and fragrance.
- Purple ruffles basil (*O. basilicum* 'Purple Ruffles'). Large, ruffled, dark purple leaves and pinkish-purple flowers make this basil very showy in borders, annual beds, and pots.
- Genovese basil (*O. basilicum* 'Genovese'). Large-leaf type is perfect for making pesto.
- Cinnamon basil (*O. basilicum*). Greenish-bronze leaves have a purplish tinge and a distinctive cinnamon taste and aroma.
- Holy basil (*O. tenuiflorum*). So named because of its deep religious significance for people of the Hindu faith. Tastes of lemon, clove, and anise, a combination that may not appeal to everyone. Not always easy to obtain, and often incorrectly identified in nursery and catalog offerings.
- West African (or East Indian) basil (*O. gratissimum*). Musky aroma and medicinally spicy flavor are definitely an acquired taste. Makes an attractive ornamental.

Commercial field of sweet basil

BERGAMOT *Monarda didyma*
Labiatae (Lamiaceae; mint family)
Also known as: American melissa, bee balm, fragrant balm, horse mint,
Indian plume, mountain balm, Oswego tea, red balm, scarlet monarda

Zone
4
Coldest Tolerated

DESCRIPTION
- Bergamot is an arresting, highly scented perennial that grows from 60 to 120 cm (2 to 4 feet) tall, and spreads vigorously in clumps, sometimes up to 1 m (3 feet) across. A true native North American wildflower, beautiful bergamot is ideal for borders, although it does take up a lot of space when fully grown.
- Rough, dark green, paired leaves have coarsely toothed edges. The oval, pointed leaves, which droop slightly, have a pungent, lemon-like aroma and flavor, with mint undertones. Upper leaves and surrounding bracts are often tinged with red or bronze.
- Bergamot has hard, square, grooved stems, and fragile, creeping roots that do not penetrate deeply into the soil.
- Produces striking crimson or scarlet flower heads that are made up of trumpet-shaped florets, while blooms of cultivars range from lovely but less dramatic pink, purple, and white. Flowers, which have the same delightful citrus-mint aroma and flavor as the leaves, appear in midsummer.
- Bergamot is particularly attractive to hummingbirds, butterflies, and bumblebees.
- Both flowers and leaves may be eaten.

Bergamot

CULTIVATION NOTES
- Bergamot does best in rich, moist, slightly acid, well-drained, highly organic soils. Add 1 cm (½ inch) compost each spring. Recommended pH range is 5.5 to 6.5.
- Prefers slight shade, but does tolerate full sun. Plants must be kept moist during dry weather.
- Start seeds indoors, or in cold frames outdoors, about 8 weeks before your last spring frost date. Sow indoor seeds 6 mm (¼ inch) deep; outdoor seeds 1 cm (½ inch) deep.

- Plant seedlings in the garden a week after your last spring frost date. Plants grown from seeds sometimes don't flower the first year.
- Can also be propagated by dividing mature plants in early spring. Take divisions from the outer, more vigorous parts of the clump, and transplant them slightly deeper than the mother plants.
- Bergamot spreads by a large number of underground stolons, which are produced each fall. In 3 or 4 years, a clump of bergamot can expand to more than 1 m (3 feet), as the underground runners spread out from the center and send up new stems. To contain bergamot's expansive growth, plant it in a pot in the

Bergamot

ground, or restrain it with a plastic or metal "collar" that extends from above ground to 2.5 cm (1 inch) below the earth.
- After 3 or 4 years, the central stems begin to lose their vigor. To renew the plant's attractive appearance, dig up the center of the clump and replant with vigorous divisions from the periphery.
- Allow 25 cm (10 inches) between plants.
- Usually pest-free, although aphids are sometimes a problem. Very susceptible to powdery mildew. Providing the plants with good air circulation helps prevent this problem. Use pine needles as mulch rather than lawn clippings, as pine needles allow air to circulate at ground level and hold less moisture. Cut affected plants back to 8 cm (3 inches) after blooming. Burn damaged leaves and stems to destroy the overwintering stages of the fungus.
- Overwinters outdoors up to zone 4. Mulch well to protect the shallow roots. Make sure the soil does not become compacted in the winter months, as this will kill the roots.

> *The genus Monarda is named after the Spanish medical botanist, Nicholas de Monardes (1493–1588), who first wrote about the plant's medicinal properties in his book on medicinal flora of North America entitled Joyfull Newes out of the Newe Founde Worlde.*

HARVESTING NOTES

- Pick leaves for fresh use at any time, ideally in the morning after the dew has evaporated.
- Collect leaves and blooms for drying in midsummer. Spread out the leaves on a wire rack in a shady, warm, ventilated location. If the leaves haven't dried in 2 or 3 days, place them

on a cookie sheet in a warm oven, as they must dry quickly to retain color and flavor. When dry, crush the leaves and store in an airtight container in the dark.
- Pick flowers when blooms are almost completely open, then hang to dry.
- Freeze flowers and freshly chopped leaves for later use.
- For dried floral arrangements, leave at least 30 cm (12 inches) of stem below the blooms.

> *Bergamot is sometimes called Oswego tea after the tribe of Native Americans who lived in what is now upstate New York, and who used the plant extensively.*

CULINARY USES
- Enliven the taste and look of salads by adding a sprinkling of bergamot flowers. Use fresh or dried leaves in tomato dishes, and as a substitute for sage in stuffing for poultry and meats, especially pork and veal.
- Bergamot leaves, fresh or dried, make a delightfully refreshing tea, reminiscent of Earl Grey. Steep 5 mL (1 teaspoon) of leaves or flowers in 250 mL (1 cup) of boiling water. Sweeten with honey to taste. For a perfect summer cooler, serve iced bergamot tea with a slice of lemon.
- Add fresh leaves and tender sprigs to wine-based drinks, fruit punch, lemonade, jellies, and fruit ices.

CRAFT USES
- Brighten floral arrangements by including fresh or dried bergamot flowers.
- Include the colorful, fragrant dried flowers in herbal wreaths and potpourris.

MEDICINAL USES
- Bergamot was used by the native peoples of North America for a wide variety of ailments, and the plant's chemical properties suggest that it may have medicinal virtues. However, as modern medical research has not yet justified recommending bergamot to treat any ailment, you should use it just for culinary and ornamental purposes.
- Bergamot contains a substance called thymol, which is used in modern medicine and dentistry as an antiseptic.

> *Early American colonists who were boycotting black tea to protest British taxes on imported tea turned to bergamot tea as a substitute. In no time, bergamot tea became the "freedom tea" of choice of pre–Revolutionary America.*

CAUTIONS
- As species of *Monarda* can stimulate menstruation and cause uterine contraction when consumed in large medicinal doses, you should avoid consuming large quantities of bergamot if you are pregnant or suffering from menstrual disorders.
- The herb "bergamot" seems to have acquired the name by having a similar fragrance to *Citrus bergamia*, a small old-world tree that produces oil used in preparing Earl Grey tea.

Concentrated "bergamot oil" from *Citrus bergamia* is sold for aromatherapy, and can be quite toxic, both externally and internally, so it should not be confused with the edible bergamot described here.

• Check cut flowers to make sure there are no bumblebees on the blooms.

> *American settlers used bergamot oil to perfume hair tonics made from bear grease.*

CULTIVARS AND RELATIVES

There are 16 species of bergamot. Any of these fragrant beauties will make a delightful addition to your herb garden:

Wild bergamot × Bergamot hybrid

• Wild bergamot (*M. fistulosa*). Very fragrant with an oregano-like taste. Ideal for flavoring semi-soft ricotta cheese, meat, and wild game. Attractive ornamental has lavender flowers that attract bumblebees. Often found along roadsides, in dry thickets, and borders of woods.
• Lemon bergamot (*M. citriodora*). Charming ornamental annual, with white, purplish, or pink- and purple-dotted flowers in pagoda-like whorls. Lemon-scented foliage with thyme overtones. Makes excellent tea. Add young leaves to salads and fruit punches, or use as a garnish.
• 'Marshall's Delight,' a hybrid of *M. fistulosa* and *M. didyma*. Pretty pink blooms. Resistant to powdery mildew.
• 'Petite Delight'(*M. fistulosa*). Compact strain that grows only 25 to 30 cm (10 to 12 inches) tall. Ideal for small urban gardens. Produces masses of lavender-pink flowers. Resistant to powdery mildew.

> *Native North Americans used to apply crushed leaves of wild bergamot to reduce the sting and itching associated with insect bites, hence the common name "bee balm." Despite the common name, however, bee balms often do not make good forage for bees, as the deep-throated flowers of many of the species, especially M. fistulosa, are too difficult for bees smaller than bumblebees to enter and reach the nectar.*

Lemon bergamot

BORAGE *Borago officinalis*
Boraginaceae (borage family)
Also known as: Bee bread, bee plant, burage, cool tankard, ox-tongue, star flower, tailwort

Annual

DESCRIPTION
- Borage is a hardy annual (occasionally biennial) whose lovely drooping flowers make it ideal for rock gardens. This robust native of the northeast Mediterranean can grow from 15 cm (6 inches) to more than 1 m (3 feet) tall.
- Plant first produces a rosette of leaves out of which a branching, flowering stem (sometimes several stems) emerges.
- Oval, gray-green leaves are hairy and pointed. The young leaves have a delectably salty, cucumber-like taste.
- Borage has round, hollow, prickly stems, and a taproot.
- Produces a profusion of pretty star-shaped flowers from midsummer through early fall. Usually blue, but sometimes white, violet, or reddish-purple, the flowers have a cucumbery taste, and are about 2 cm (¾ inch) in diameter. Flowers have a distinctive cone of black anthers in the center of each bloom, and a high nectar content that makes them extremely attractive to honeybees.
- May be grown in pots, both indoors and outdoors.
- Both leaves and flowers may be eaten.

CULTIVATION NOTES
- Borage is tolerant of many soil types, but does not like heavy, poorly drained soil. Tolerated pH range is 4.3 to 8.5, which is unusually wide. A pH of 6.0 to 7.0 is recommended.
- Prefers full sunlight, but will grow in partial shade. Although borage can withstand dry conditions, it does best in soil with average moisture.
- Likes cool growing conditions and is frost-tolerant.

45

- Plant seeds directly in the garden where you want the plants to grow, as borage does not transplant well. Seeds need light to germinate, so plant no more than 6 mm (¼ inch) deep. Seedlings emerge in 5 to 8 days. Keep the soil moist while the plants are young.
- Space plants 30 to 50 cm (12 to 20 inches) apart.
- For a constant supply of fresh young leaves, sow a new row of seeds every few weeks.
- Once established in the garden, borage self-sows abundantly. Thin new seedlings as required.
- Susceptible to infestations of painted lady butterfly, tarnished plant bug, wooly bear caterpillar, and flea beetle, and to crown rot of the stems and leaf spot.
- When cultivating borage in pots, sow seeds in the containers in which plants are to grow.
- Indoor plants prefer cool temperatures, although they do need to be grown in a sunny window or they will become leggy. Water and fertilize lightly.

> *Charles Dickens is reputed to have been particularly fond of borage punch, a rather potent concoction of sherry, brandy, apple cider, lemon, sugar, and borage flowers.*

HARVESTING NOTES
- Harvest young leaves for fresh use throughout the growing season. As harvested leaves wilt quickly, pick them just before you intend to use them.
- Pick flowers, either individually or in clusters, when they're fully open and quite dry, usually around midmorning.
- Borage is not suitable for drying as the leaves lose their flavor and color.
- If grown indoors, harvest the young leaves regularly like spinach.

CULINARY USES
- Add the flowers and finely chopped, fresh young leaves to your favorite salads.
- Steam leaves and flowers as you would spinach or Swiss chard.
- Use young leaves in soup, as a flavoring for yogurt, in curries, and in fish and chicken dishes.
- Make a refreshing tea by pouring 250 mL (1 cup) boiling water over 15 mL (1 tablespoon) of crushed fresh leaves.
- Float the flowers on a cool summer drink or punch for a pretty presentation.
- Candy the flowers and use for decorating cakes and ice cream.

> *In medieval times, borage flowers were embroidered on the scarves of warriors to aid them in battle. The herb was reputed to promote courage, as exemplified in the old motto, "I borage, bring always courage."*

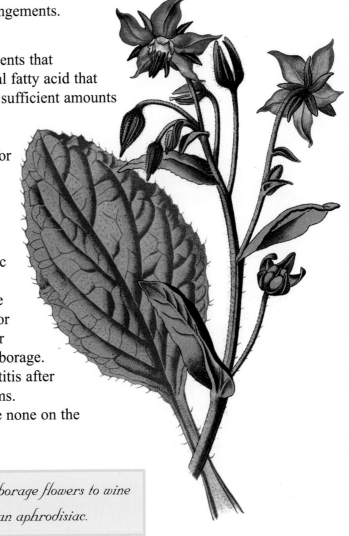

Borage is likely the herb the Greek poet Homer called nepenthe, which resulted in blissful forgetfulness when drunk in wine.

CRAFT USES
• Include pretty borage in fresh floral arrangements.

MEDICINAL USES
• Borage seeds are used in health supplements that supply gamma linolenic acid, an essential fatty acid that some individuals are unable to obtain in sufficient amounts from a normal diet.
• Because borage contains soothing mucilage, it makes a relieving poultice for skin inflammations.
• Young leaves are rich in potassium, calcium, vitamin C, and beta-carotene.

CAUTIONS
• Borage contains small amounts of a toxic chemical, so while eating it in moderation is harmless, consuming large quantities is unwise. If you're pregnant or nursing, or if you suffer from epilepsy or schizophrenia, you should not consume borage.
• Some people experience bouts of dermatitis after touching the hairs on the leaves and stems.
• Bees love borage, so be careful there are none on the flowers you pick.

According to Lebanese custom, adding borage flowers to wine turns the fruit of the grape into an aphrodisiac.

CARAWAY *Carum carvi*
Umbelliferae (Apiaceae; carrot family)
Also known as: Common caraway, Roman cumin

Zone 3 Coldest Tolerated

DESCRIPTION

- Caraway, an ancient culinary herb used since the Stone Age, is a biennial that is sometimes grown as an annual. When grown as a biennial, this native of Europe, western Asia, and northern Africa reaches about 20 cm (8 inches) in the first year and generally about 0.6 m (2 feet) in the second year, although plants in flower can grow up to 1.5 m (5 feet).
- Light green, aromatic, fern-like leaves are finely divided and have a flavor reminiscent of dill, to which caraway is related.
- Caraway has hollow, grooved, branched stems, and a fleshy, white, carrot-shaped root.
- Biennial caraway cultivars produce flat umbels of tiny, greenish-white flowers that bloom in late summer in the plant's second year. The blossoms, which resemble those of Queen Anne's lace, appear on stems above the plant's foliage.
- Flowers are followed by flat, oblong seeds or fruits, which are dark brown when ripe.
- Both the seeds and roots have a distinctive, sharp, spicy flavor and fragrance.
- Leaves, seeds, and roots may all be eaten.

CULTIVATION NOTES

- Caraway grows best in well-tilled, moderately light clay soil that is rich in humus. Tolerated pH range is 4.8 to 7.8.
- Needs full sunlight and requires additional watering during dry spells.

48

- Sow seeds directly in the garden in early spring, as soon as the soil can be worked. Seeds are slow to germinate. (Putting seeds in the freezer for a few days before planting may improve germination.)
- Plant seeds about 6 mm (¼ inch) deep. Seedlings usually emerge in 8 to 12 days.
- Space plants 20 cm (8 inches) apart. (You only need a few plants for a good supply of seeds.)
- Although caraway self-seeds, the resulting plants may be rather weedy.
- Susceptible to crown rot, and to infestations of aphids and carrot weevils.
- Overwinters outdoors up to zone 3.

Pair of mature seeds

> *The ancient Arabs, who used caraway extensively as a spice and flavoring, called the seeds* karawya *or* karauya, *names that are still in use for caraway seeds in some parts of the Middle East.*

HARVESTING NOTES
- Harvest fresh leaves at any time after the plants are about 15 cm (6 inches) high.
- Harvest seeds when they have ripened, but before they fall to the ground. Cut leaf stems (with seed heads) at the base. Enclose the seed heads in a paper bag to catch the ripe seeds as they fall, then hang the stems upside down in a warm, dry location. When the seeds are dry, shake the heads vigorously. Be sure seeds are thoroughly dry before storing them in airtight jars.
- Harvest roots in the fall.

> *In the 1ˢᵗ century AD, the Greek physician Dioscorides prescribed a caraway tonic for young girls of pallid complexion in the belief that it would restore color to their cheeks.*

CULINARY USES
- Add fresh young caraway leaves to soups, stews, and salads. Try cooking the older leaves like spinach, but be prepared for a stronger, spicier flavor, like that of the seeds.
- Cook the roots and serve them as you would carrots or parsnips.
- Caraway seeds are widely used to flavor and season rye breads, cakes (they are a fine substitute for poppy seeds in old standbys such as seed cake), biscuits, cheeses, omelets, pasta, soups, salad dressing, applesauce, rice, and seafood. Vegetable dishes using beets, carrots, potatoes, green beans, cauliflower, cucumber, onions, zucchini, and turnips often call for the addition of caraway seeds. Coleslaw and sauerkraut, and indeed all cabbage dishes, are incomplete without caraway seeds. (If you don't like the smell of cooking cabbage, put a 5 mL (1 teaspoon) of caraway seeds in a muslin bag and boil it with the cabbage.)
- The essential oil from caraway seeds is used commercially to flavor pickles, marinades, preserved meats, confectionery, condiments, candy, ice cream, and alcoholic beverages such as aquavit and kümmel.

> *Julius Caesar is said to have been particularly fond of a caraway seed bread called* chara.

> *Reference is made to caraway in a venerable old cookbook compiled by the master cooks of England's King Richard II in about 1390. By the Elizabethan period, caraway was widely used in English cooking. In Shakespeare's Henry IV, Part II, Falstaff is invited to partake of "a pippin. . .with a dish of caraways."*

MEDICINAL USES

- In traditional folk medicine and in modern medicine in some European countries, caraway seeds are recommended to relieve gas and flatulence and as a treatment for indigestion. Caraway tea, made by infusing 5 mL (1 teaspoon) of ground or crushed seed in 250 mL (1 cup) of boiling water, has long been a popular remedy for digestive upsets.
- Caraway oil is used in the pharmaceutical industry in medicines, mouthwashes, and gargles. The oil is also used in making soap and perfume.

> *According to German folklore, sprinkling caraway seeds in the coffin of a loved one protects the departed from sorcerers and hexes, while bread made with caraway seeds is said to drive away demons.*

CAUTIONS

- Commercial caraway oil should be handled only by experts. Some people may experience dermatitis from contact with the essential oil.

> *Pigeon fanciers sometimes put caraway dough in the birds' lofts in the belief that this will prevent the birds from wandering off.*

CATNIP *Nepeta cataria*

Labiatae (Lamiaceae; mint family)
Also known as: Catmint, catnep, catrup, catwort, English catnip,
field balm, nep, nip

Zone
3
Coldest
Tolerated

DESCRIPTION

- Catnip, a hardy perennial that grows 0.6 to 1 m (2 to 3 feet) tall, is native from the eastern Mediterranean region to the western Himalayas, central Asia, southern Siberia, and China. Most cats love catnip and purr contentedly, tear delightedly, and roll in ecstasy on its crushed leaves.
- Light green, scalloped, opposite leaves have heart-shaped bases, pointed tips, and velvety, grayish-white undersides. The edible leaves, which have a strong mint-like, warm, pungent, bitterish fragrance and flavor, grow in massed profusion before the plant flowers. After the blossoms appear, the leaves become more sparse.
- Catnip has erect, square, branching stems that are covered in soft hairs. The root becomes quite woody and branched with age. Each spring the root sends up an increasing number of new stems, many of which are rather close together.
- Produces spikes of small whitish or pinkish, purple- or red-dotted flowers in midsummer.
- May be grown indoors for winter use.
- Catnip is an excellent honey plant.

CULTIVATION NOTES

- Catnip grows bushiest in well-drained, moderately rich soil, although it also grows well in dry, sandy soil. Add a light layer of compost to the top of the soil before planting. Recommended pH range is 4.9 to 7.5.

51

- Thrives in partial shade, but can be grown in full sun.
- Grows easily from seed, which should be started indoors about 6 to 8 weeks before your last spring frost date. Sow seeds no more than 6 mm (¼ inch) deep. Seedlings usually emerge in 8 to 10 days.
- Space transplanted seedlings 30 cm (12 inches) apart.
- Can also be propagated by dividing the roots in the spring or fall, or from softwood or stem tip cuttings. Cuttings from young plants tend to root more quickly, often in just a week. Stem cuttings should be about 10 cm (4 inches) long. Grow rooted cuttings to about 15 cm (6 inches) in a moist medium before you transplant them to the garden.
- Catnip self-sows easily, so be prepared to remove unwanted plants. Weed as required.
- For bushier plants, pinch flower buds as they appear.
- Usually pest-free, but susceptible to rust and root rot.
- Cats are the biggest problem confronting catnip gardeners. Give young plants a chance to get established by enclosing them in a sturdy chicken wire cage, which will protect them from enthusiastic felines. Cats are drawn to catnip only when the branches are broken or the leaves are bruised, thereby releasing the attractant chemicals, so if the plants aren't damaged, cats will probably leave them alone.
- Overwinters outdoors up to zone 3.
- Indoor plants should be potted in moist, but not soggy soil that is supplemented with lime. Plants need at least 5 hours of direct sunlight daily. Prune as required, as plants are inclined to become scraggly.

> *The generic name Nepeta comes from the Italian town Nepete, where catnip was once cultivated.*

HARVESTING NOTES
- Pick leaves for fresh use at any time throughout the summer, although the taste is milder if you pick the leaves before the plant flowers. Collect the leaves in the morning, after the dew has evaporated.
- To dry catnip, harvest complete stems, including the flowering head and the tender leaves. Cut stems about 5 cm (2 inches) from the ground, and hang upside down in a shady location. When dry, strip off the leaves, crumble them, and store in airtight jars out of the light.

CULINARY USES
- Catnip was a familiar herb in English kitchen gardens as far back as the 13th century. Catnip leaves were once used for rubbing meats before they were cooked, and were chopped and sprinkled into green salads. Snip a few leaves into your salads and see how you like it.
- Add fresh or dried leaves to soups, stews, and hearty sauces.

- Make a refreshing, soothing cup of tea by pouring 250 mL (1 cup) of boiling water over 15 mL (3 teaspoons) of fresh leaves or 5 mL (1 teaspoon) of dried leaves. Alternatively, add dried catnip leaves, along with dried mint or dried lemon balm, to your favorite black tea.

CRAFT USES
- Sew cat toys and stuff them with uncrushed dry leaves for all your favorite felines.

MEDICINAL USES
- In traditional folk medicine, catnip was used to treat everything from cancer, insanity, nervousness, nightmares, scurvy, and tuberculosis, to colic, diarrhea, flatulence, hiccups, whooping cough, the common cold, measles, asthma, yellow fever, scarlet fever, smallpox, and jaundice. Catnip poultices were applied to hives, and to the sore breasts of nursing mothers.
- Catnip does have sedative qualities and is occasionally used in herbal medicine as a calmative and to treat insomnia.
- Catnip is not used in modern Western medicine.

> *While most cats are affected by catnip, not all felines are "nipaholics." Apparently, a dominant gene is responsible for inheriting the euphoric response. It also appears that cats do not react in their customary delighted way to catnip until they are 3 months old.*

CAUTIONS
- Catnip has some capacity to cause uterine contractions and stimulate menstruation, so you should avoid it if you are pregnant or suffering from menstrual disorders.
- While a cup of catnip tea is helpful if you don't sleep well at night, the herb's diuretic properties mean that your peaceful sleep may be disturbed by an urgent need to go to the bathroom.
- It has been said that catnip may be smoked like marijuana; however, there is no proof that this herb has the intoxicating effects of marijuana. Nevertheless, your suspicions may be justified if young people of your acquaintance seem unusually interested in your catnip plants.
- Bees like catnip, so make sure there are none in the flowers that you pick.

CULTIVARS AND RELATIVES
Here's a cultivar you won't have to fight over with your cats quite so much.
- Lemon catnip (*N. cataria* var. *citriodora*). Has an appealingly mild lemon aroma, which you may prefer over regular catnip. Makes a delicious tea. When candied with egg white and sugar, the leaves make a refreshing after-dinner mint.

> *In the belief that catnip roots made even the kindest person mean, early American hangmen used to eat the roots before executions to harden themselves for their work.*

CHAMOMILE Compositae (Asteraceae; sunflower family)

GERMAN CHAMOMILE
Matricaria recutita

Also known as: Common chamomile, false chamomile, Hungarian chamomile, matricaria, sweet false chamomile, wild chamomile

ROMAN CHAMOMILE
Chamaemelum nobile

Also known as: English chamomile, garden chamomile, lawn chamomile, manzanilla, noble chamomile, Russian chamomile, white chamomile

Annual

Zone 3
Coldest Tolerated

DESCRIPTION

German chamomile

- The chamomiles are among the most popular of all herbs used for making tea. German chamomile is a sweet-scented, upright annual that grows 0.6 to 1 m (2 to 3 feet) tall. Equally aromatic Roman chamomile, a low-growing, trailing perennial – at least the root system is perennial – ranges from 10 to 30 cm (4 to 12 inches) in height. German chamomile is native to Europe and western Asia; Roman chamomile is a native of western Europe, the Azores, and North Africa.
- German chamomile has feathery, bright green, fern-like leaves. Roman chamomile has finely divided, parsley-like leaves that are flatter and thicker than those of German chamomile.
- German chamomile has smooth, branched, erect stems. Roman chamomile has creeping, many-branched, hairy stems, and a fibrous root.
- Both chamomiles produce small, daisy-like white blossoms with yellow centers. The chamomiles bloom in midsummer, with Roman chamomile usually flowering first.
- The chamomiles have a delightfully light aroma and taste that is redolent of apple.
- Both flowers and leaves may be eaten.

CULTIVATION NOTES

- German chamomile grows well in poor, clay soil, while Roman chamomile does best in well-drained, slightly acidic, moderately fertile soil. Tolerated pH range for German chamomile is 4.5 to 7.5; for Roman chamomile, the tolerated pH range is 5.5 to 8.0.
- Roman chamomile does not do well in hot, dry weather.

54

- Both chamomiles thrive in open, sunny locations, but will grow in light shade.
- Grow both types from seed, which should be sown in the garden in spring. Sow seeds shallowly to a depth of 6 mm (¼ inch) or less. Keep ground moist and free of weeds. Seedlings usually appear in 5 to 10 days.
- Roman chamomile can also be propagated easily by separating the runners and replanting them.
- Space German chamomile about 10 cm (4 inches) apart and Roman chamomile about 45 cm (18 inches) apart. German chamomile seedlings transplant best when plants are young and no more than 5 cm (2 inches) tall.
- Both types are mostly pest- and disease-free.
- Once established, German chamomile self-sows readily, so you'll likely have a fresh crop the following year. Roman chamomile can overwinter outdoors as far north as zone 3.

Chamomile comes from the Greek kamai, meaning "on the ground," and melon, meaning "apple," reflecting the apple-like aroma and low growing habit of Roman chamomile. In Spanish, chamomile is known as manzanilla, meaning "little apple," and the Spanish light sherry of the same name is flavored with chamomile.

HARVESTING NOTES
- Harvest flowers of both types for drying and for fresh use when they are fully open. Don't delay harvesting Roman chamomile, as the flowers lose their flavor once they start to darken.
- To dry both chamomiles, snip the flowers off with scissors, then rinse and pat dry. Place flower heads on a rack or mesh screen and set to dry in a warm location. When flowers are completely dry, store in jars in the dark.
- Harvest fresh leaves as needed.

CULINARY USES

It is estimated that the worldwide daily consumption of chamomile tea exceeds one million cups.

- Use fresh or dried chamomile flowers to brew delectable herbal tea. Deciding which chamomile to use is a matter of personal taste. German chamomile is sweeter than Roman chamomile, which has a slightly bitter bite. Whatever your choice, both make excellent tea.
- To make chamomile tea, infuse 15 mL (1 tablespoon) of fresh flowers or 10 mL (2 teaspoons) of dried flowers in 250 mL (1 cup) of boiling water. Steep for 5 to 10 minutes.
- Strew a few Roman chamomile flowers over a tossed green salad, and season cream sauces, butter, and sour cream by adding small sprigs of either type.
- Both German and Roman chamomile are used commercially to flavor alcoholic beverages, such as Benedictine and vermouth, and confectionery, candy, ice cream, baked goods, desserts, and chewing gum.

Readers of Beatrix Potter's The Tale of Peter Rabbit will recall that Mother Rabbit made Peter a soothing cup of chamomile tea after his harrowing adventures in Mr. McGregor's garden.

CRAFT USES

- Add fragrant chamomile flowers to potpourris and sachets.

MEDICINAL USES

Roman chamomile

- In traditional folk medicine, both types were widely used as sedatives and tonics. Chamomile was also used to treat asthma, colic, fever, flatulence, heartburn, inflammations, menstrual problems, hemorrhoids, toothache, earache, and cancer, while poultices of Roman chamomile were recommended for neuralgia sufferers.
- While chamomile's curative powers are limited, it is one of the safest of the traditional medicinal herbs. Chamomile does have mild sedative ability and it can help to reduce gastrointestinal upsets.
- In modern medicine, Roman chamomile is used in antiseptic lotions and to flavor pharmaceutical products.
- Chamomile is used commercially in a number of personal care products including cosmetics, hair color, mouthwash, and sunscreen. It is also used in shampoos and conditioners to bring out the highlights in blond hair, and as a moisturizer for dry hair.

During the Middle Ages, Roman chamomile was a popular strewing herb, purposely planted in walks so that when it was stepped on, it released its lovely aroma.

CAUTIONS

- People who are allergic to ragweed may also have an allergic reaction to chamomile, but this is rare.
- Chamomile is sometimes consumed in very large doses for medicinal purposes. If you are pregnant or nursing, you should not take large medicinal quantities of chamomile.
- Avoid using chamomile preparations for teething babies.

Roman chamomile has long been a popular ground cover as it stands up well to traffic. It is likely the chamomile referred to by Falstaff in Shakespeare's Henry IV, Part I: "the chamomile, the more it is trodden on, the faster it grows." And Sir Francis Drake is believed to have been playing bowls on a green of Roman chamomile when told that the Spanish Armada was approaching the English Channel.

CULTIVARS AND RELATIVES

- Treneague chamomile (*C. nobile* 'Treneague'). Non-flowering form of Roman chamomile makes attractive ground cover and can be mown. Unfortunately, it lacks chamomile's distinctive scent and is not winter-hardy.

The ancient Egyptians considered German chamomile to be a sacred gift from Ra, the sun god, to be used to alleviate the effects of high fevers and sunstroke.

CHERVIL *Anthriscus cerefolium*

Umbelliferae (Apiaceae; carrot family)

Also known as: Beaked parsley, French parsley, garden chervil, gourmet parsley, salad chervil

DESCRIPTION

- Chervil, a dainty annual that grows from 30 to 45 cm (12 to 18 inches) tall, is native to southern Russia, the Caucasus, and perhaps the Middle East. Under the right conditions, plants may spread out to twice their height.
- The finely divided leaves resemble parsley, but are a lighter green and more feathery. There are both curly and flat-leaved forms. Foliage has a subtle anise flavor and fragrance, with a slight hint of pepper.
- Chervil has thin, erect stems, and shallow roots.
- Produces tiny white flowers in clusters similar to Queen Anne's lace. Blooms in early summer.
- Grows well in pots, and may be cultivated indoors for winter use.
- Leaves, flowers, and roots may all be eaten.

CULTIVATION NOTES

- Chervil grows best in rich, loamy, well-drained soils that are slightly acidic, neutral, or slightly alkaline. Tolerated pH range is 5.0 to 8.2.
- Prefers partial shade.
- Chervil does not like heat and will bolt (flower and set seed) during hot, dry weather. Also intolerant of high humidity. Prefers cool spring or fall growing conditions, and withstands light frost.
- Sow seeds outdoors about 2 weeks before your last spring frost date. As chervil has delicate roots and does not transplant well, sow seeds in fine soil where the plants are to grow. Seeds should be fresh, as they are only viable for a short time.
- Plant seeds to 6 mm (¼ inch) or less. Seedlings usually emerge in 7 to 14 days. Keep the soil evenly moist until after germination.
- Plant new seeds every few weeks to ensure a constant supply of fresh leaves throughout the growing season.

- Space plants about 25 cm (10 inches) apart.
- May develop leaf spot in hot, humid weather. Susceptible to carrot weevils and aphids.
- Indoor plants need 4 to 5 hours of direct sunlight or 12 hours of strong artificial light daily, and cool temperatures of no more than 16°C (60°F).

> *Chervil may just be the elixir of youth. According to popular legend, it will make you merry, sharpen your wits, improve your failing memory, and restore your youthful zest.*

HARVESTING NOTES
- Begin picking outside leaves when plant is about 15 cm (6 inches) tall. Continue harvesting the leaves throughout the growing season, as frequent harvesting encourages new leaf growth.
- Pick the leaves just before use, as they wilt quickly and don't store well.
- Freeze finely chopped, fresh, young leaves in a little water in ice cube trays.
- Drying chervil is not recommended, as the leaves lose their flavor and aroma.

CULINARY USES

- Use young chervil leaves in soups, salads, stews, seafood, egg dishes, and in béchamel and ravigote sauces. Essential in tabbouleh, and delicious with chives in warm potato salad. Always add leaves to your favorite recipe at the last minute for maximum flavor and aroma.
- Chervil is often used to intensify the flavor of other herbs, and is included in the classic French *fines herbes*, along with parsley, chives, and tarragon.
- Add finely chopped leaves to butter to make a delectable spread for fish while it is cooking, or when ready to serve.
- Use leaves as a garnish for vegetable dishes, especially beans and peas, and pork dishes.
- Include flowers and leaves in stuffing.
- Cook roots and serve hot or cold as a vegetable.
- Flavor extra-virgin olive oil by adding fresh leaves.

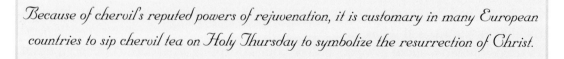

> *Because of chervil's reputed powers of rejuvenation, it is customary in many European countries to sip chervil tea on Holy Thursday to symbolize the resurrection of Christ.*

MEDICINAL USES
- Although chervil has never been widely employed as a medicinal herb, it was used in traditional herbal medicine as an expectorant and general stimulant, and to treat eczema, relieve stomach problems, and lower blood pressure. It is not used in modern medicine.
- Chervil is high in calcium.

CHIVES Liliaceae (lily family)

CHIVES
Allium schoenoprasum

Also known as: Chive, cive, civegarlic, civet ezo-negi, common garden chives, onion chives

GARLIC CHIVES
A. tuberosum

Also known as: Chinese chives, gow choy, ku ts'ai, nira, Oriental garlic

Zone
3
Coldest
Tolerated

Zone
4
Coldest
Tolerated

DESCRIPTION

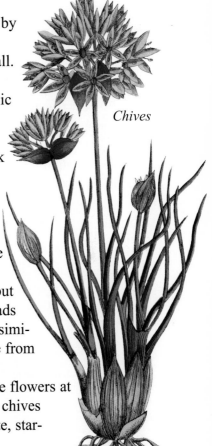

Chives

- Chives, collected from the wild since antiquity and cultivated by gardeners since the Middle Ages, is a hardy, spreading, herbaceous perennial that grows to about 70 cm (28 inches) tall. It is native to northern North America and Eurasia. Garlic chives, a native of Asia, is not as winter-hardy as chives. Garlic chives grows about 50 cm (20 inches) tall, and makes a very pretty perennial border.

- Chives has slim, dark green, hollow leaves that rise from thick tufts. Leaves have a delicate onion flavor and fragrance. Slender, white-sheathed bulbs develop in dense masses at the base of the plant, and thin roots emerge from the base of the bulbs.

- Garlic chives' leaves are flat, solid, and paler green than those of chives, and taste and smell of mild garlic, with a sweetish undertone. Some types of garlic chives produce some bulbs, but many do not, or produce only small bulbs. Garlic chives spreads by means of rhizomes (underground stems), which are rather similar to the rhizomes of the common bearded iris. Roots emerge from the underside of these rhizomes.

- Chives produces small, round clusters of rose-purple or mauve flowers at the end of a leafless stalk. Plants bloom in mid-spring. Garlic chives bloom in late summer, producing loose clusters of small, white, star-shaped florets.

- Chives may be grown indoors for winter use. As garlic chives tends to go dormant during the winter, potting for indoor use is not recommended.

- Flowers and leaves of both chives and garlic chives may be eaten, as may the bulbs of garlic chives.

CULTIVATION NOTES

- Chives and garlic chives grow in most soils, but both do best in well-drained, organic, fertile soil. Tolerated pH range for chives is 5.0 to 8.2; for garlic chives, the pH range is 4.5 to 8.3.
- Both types grow best in full sun, but chives does tolerate light shade. Keep soil moist throughout the growing season. (Cut back on watering garlic chives during the first season to promote root growth.)
- Chives and garlic chives are best started by dividing existing clumps. Divide in spring or fall.
- Both types may also be grown from seed, which should be started indoors in fiber pots about 8 weeks before your last spring frost date. Plant seeds to a depth of 6 mm (¼ inch) or less. Seeds need darkness to germinate. Seedlings usually appear in 7 to 12 days. To establish a clump of chives quickly, transplant several seedlings together.
- Chives and garlic chives can be grown as annuals, but they grow slowly and don't provide a large harvest the first year.
- Space clumps of plants 30 cm (12 inches) apart.
- Lift and divide established beds of chives every 3 years or so, as division prevents over-crowding and stops the central portion of the plants from dying out. Cut away flower stalks to prevent reseeding, and to maintain vigorous leaf growth.
- Prune garlic chives' shoots back to within 2.5 cm (1 inch) of the ground if the plants become woody.
- Generally pest-free, but susceptible to fungus diseases in overcrowded, soggy conditions.
- Chives can overwinter outdoors as far north as zone 3. Garlic chives overwinters outdoors up to zone 4, providing it is well mulched.
- Pot chives for indoor use in late summer. Transplant a clump into a 13-cm (5 inch) pot, buried in the ground. Leave outside until the first heavy fall frost kills off the tops of the plant. Trim off the dead tops, dig up the pot, and put in a cool location for about 3 months. At the end of this dormancy period, set the pot in a sunny windowsill. Keep watered.

Garlic chives

The species name schoenoprasum *comes from the Greek* skhoinos, *meaning "rush," and* prason, *meaning "leek," a reference to chives' rush–like leaves.*

HARVESTING NOTES

- Pick chives any time during the growing season after the leaves are about 15 cm (6 inches) long. Pick only the leaves, as the flower stalks may be tough.
- Harvest chives by hand, picking the leaves off at the base. Don't cut the leaves with scissors, as the resulting dieback has an unattractive brown edge.
- Chives is best used fresh. Although the leaves can be frozen in ice cubes for later use, dried chives lack both color and flavor.
- Pick chives flowers when they are just fully open.
- Avoid harvesting garlic chives in the first year to enable the plant to develop a good root system. Thereafter, pick the leaves as required once they are about 15 cm (6 inches) long. Garlic chives leaves are very soft and quickly lose freshness. Like chives, they may be frozen, but should not be dried.
- Pick the flower buds of garlic chives for fresh use or for drying. Flower stems are also edible.

In Taiwan, it is customary to shelter garlic chives under a sort of mini pup tent made out of bamboo and straw mats. Keeping light off the leaves in this way blanches them and makes them more tender.

CULINARY USES

- Use tender, mild chives leaves to season cream cheese and butter, and in salads, soups, vegetables, sauces, egg dishes, meat and poultry, and seafood –especially salmon, caviar, and oysters.
- Garnish salads, entrees, and hot and cold soups with a sprinkling of freshly snipped chives. (No bowl of vichyssoise is ready to serve without chives.)
- When cooking with chives, add it to your dish during the last 5 to 10 minutes, as prolonged heat destroys the flavor.
- Add leaves to vinegar and extra-virgin olive oil.
- Try the flowers in egg, cheese, and fish dishes, or use as a garnish. As the pungent flavor of an entire flower head can be overwhelming, break it into individual florets, and add discretely until you find your flavor tolerance level.
- Use the leaves of garlic chives as you would those of chives, but expect a stronger, sharper flavor. When cooking with garlic chives, add just before serving, as the leaves lose flavor and become stringy if overcooked.

Chives

- Garlic chives is a staple of Asian cooking. Only fresh leaves are used, and are typically fried with vegetables and meat. Garlic chives is essential for Japanese miso soup.
- Use the small bulbs of garlic chives as you would garlic, especially in recipes calling for a more delicate flavor than true garlic.

- Eat garlic chives flower buds as you would those of chives. Flower stems may also be used for seasoning.
- Chives is used commercially in soup mixes, salad dressings, savory dips, sour cream, and cottage cheese.

> *Chives was so popular in 19th century Holland that farmers apparently fed it to their cattle in order to have the animals produce chives–flavored milk.*

CRAFT USES
- Include the purple pompoms of chives and the showy white flowers of garlic chives in summer bouquets of fresh flowers.

MEDICINAL USES
- Chives was used in traditional folk medicine to treat intestinal parasites, enhance the immune system, stimulate digestion, and treat anemia.
- In Chinese herbal medicine, garlic chives has long been used to treat fatigue, help control excessive bleeding, and as an antidote for ingested poisons. The leaves and bulbs are applied to insect bites, cuts, and wounds, while the seeds are used to treat kidney, liver, and digestive system problems.
- Both chives and garlic chives are rich in vitamin C. Chives leaves are a good source of fiber, potassium, and vitamin A. Garlic chives is high in carotene, thiamine, and riboflavin. Garlic chives is also rich in minerals, especially calcium and iron.

CAUTIONS
- Chives may cause dermatitis in some people.

> *Widespread mythology has it that a bunch of chives suspended from the ceiling or hung from the bedpost wards off evil spirits or the evil eye.*

CULTIVARS AND RELATIVES
- Egyptian onion (*A.* × *proliferum*). Natural hybrid between common onion (*A. cepa* L) and Japanese bunching onion (*A. fistulosum* L). Grows up to 1 m (3 feet) tall. Bulbils or topsets are initially green, changing to brownish-red, and are about the size of hazelnuts. Produces sideshoots or offsets from the base of the plant. Sideshoots may be eaten raw or cooked. Use the new green leaf tips as a garnish. White lower stalks make a fine substitute for salad onions. Thin the stalks from the parent plant and use them instead of scallions. Eat the bulbils, either raw or cooked, if you like an intense onion flavor. Pickle the bulbils as you would onions.
- Windowsill chives (*A. schoenoprasum* 'Grolau'). Excellent for indoor winter cultivation. Strong flavor with thick, dark, green leaves that should be trimmed continuously to maintain vigorous growth.

Egyptian onion

62

CICELY, SWEET *Myrrhis odorata*

Umbelliferae (Apiaceae; carrot family)

Also known as: Anise fern, British myrrh, cow chervil, garden myrrh, shepherd's needle, smooth cicely, sweet bracken, sweet fern, sweet chervil, sweet myrrh

Zone **4**

Coldest Tolerated

DESCRIPTION

- Sweet cicely, a robust, aromatic perennial native to the mountainous regions of Europe and Asian Russia, grows from 0.6 to 0.9 m (2 to 3 feet) tall. One of the first herbs to appear in the spring, sweet cicely makes a becoming backdrop to a perennial border.
- Soft, silky, fern-like leaves are pale green with whitish undersides, turning to purple in fall. The leaves have a distinctive sugary taste, with just a hint of licorice. The fragrance is similar to that of anise.
- Sweet cicely has hollow, furrowed stems, and a large, thick, deeply growing root.
- Seeds, which follow the flowers, are 2 cm (about ¾ inch) long, and are held upright on the plant. Dark brown and shiny when ripe, the seeds have a more powerful, sweetly liquorice flavor than the leaves.
- Produces clusters of small, whitish, sweet-scented flowers, similar to Queen Anne's lace. Blooms in May or June.
- Sweet cicely is attractive to honeybees.
- Stems, leaves, roots, and seeds may all be eaten.

CULTIVATION NOTES

- Sweet cicely grows best in deep, rich, loamy soils. Dig soil deeply to accommodate long taproot, and keep moist. Add 1 cm (½ inch) of compost or manure every spring. Recommended pH range is 5.5 to 6.5.
- Grows well both in full sun and shade.
- Sow seeds no more than 6 mm (¼ inch) deep in late summer, while they are still fresh. (Seed supply companies usually ship fresh seeds in July, just after they have been harvested.) Seeds germinate best after freezing during the winter months.
- May also be propagated by root division. Make sure each section of the upper root contains an eye. Divide roots in the spring.

- Space plants 0.6 m (2 feet) apart.
- Sweet cicely self-seeds around the base of the mature plant. To avoid unwanted volunteers, remove the fruiting stalks before the seeds ripen.
- Remove flowers immediately to ensure a plentiful supply of leaves.
- Usually pest- and disease-free.
- Overwinters outdoors up to zone 4.

> *The genus name Myrrhis comes from the Greek myron, meaning "perfume," while the specific name odorata stems from the Latin odorus, meaning "fragrant." The name is unusual in that both words of the binomial refer to the scented nature of sweet cicely.*

HARVESTING NOTES

- Harvest young leaves and stems for culinary use at any time. Leaves wilt quickly, so pick them just before use.
- Sweet cicely leaves are best when fresh, as they do not dry well and lose some of their flavor when frozen.
- Harvest seed heads while the seeds are still green and unripe. Collect seed heads with a small portion of stem attached. Hang upside down by the stems to dry. Store dry seeds in an airtight container.
- Dig roots as required, although this is not an easy task, as the roots are quite deep.
- Hang flowers to dry for inclusion in potpourris.

CULINARY USES

- Add fresh leaves to salads, soups, and stews, but don't include in highly seasoned dishes, as sweet cicely's delicate flavor is easily lost.
- Cook the sweet-tasting leaves with sour fruits such as rhubarb or gooseberries, and cut back on the sugar you usually add for sweetening.
- Use fresh leaves and green seeds as a substitute for sugar in fruit conserves.
- Add chopped, unripe seeds to salads, or use them to flavor whipped cream or ice cream.
- Include whole ripe seeds in cookies, cakes, and fruit pies, especially apple pies, where they may be substituted for cloves. When using sweet cicely seeds in baking, you should plan on decreasing the amount of sugar called for in your recipe.
- Eat the seeds as you would candy.
- Toss peeled, chopped roots in oil and vinegar and serve as a tasty side salad.
- Cook fresh roots and serve as you would your favorite recipe for parsnips. Add roots to flavor soups and stews.

CRAFT USES

- Include sweet-smelling dried flowers in potpourris.

> *The oil from sweet cicely seeds was once used for polishing furniture, especially oak, as it imparted a very fragrant, glossy finish.*

> *Although sweet cicely is also called "myrrh," it is not the biblical myrrh used in Jewish tradition in the making of the holy oil of the Tabernacle with which Moses anointed the sacred vessels. The myrrh of the Bible, which was also the myrrh included in the gifts the Magi brought the infant Jesus, is a gum obtained from the myrrh tree, Commiphora abyssinica.*

MEDICINAL USES

- In traditional herbal medicine, sweet cicely was used as a general tonic, a mild laxative, and an appetite stimulant. It was also believed to strengthen the lungs. Today, sweet cicely is rarely used medicinally.

CAUTIONS

- There are no known health hazards associated with sweet cicely; however, very little research has been done on the safety aspects of this herb. Until we know more, it's best to consume sweet cicely in moderation.

Sweet cicely is sometimes rubbed inside beehives to attract bees.

*C*ORIANDER *Coriandrum sativum*

Umbelliferae (Apiaceae; carrot family)

Also known as: Cilantro, culantrillo (Often the name "coriander" is applied to seed varieties, while "cilantro" is used for leaf varieties.)

DESCRIPTION

- Coriander is a strongly aromatic, erect annual that typically grows from 30 to 90 cm (1 to 3 feet) tall. This southern European and Mediterranean native is one of the world's most important spices, and is very widely used in cooking.
- The plant has 2 types of bright green, shiny leaves: the broad, toothed lower ones resemble flat parsley, while the lacy upper leaves are fern-like and have a stronger aroma. The scent and flavor of the leaves are particularly pungent and are often an acquired taste.
- Coriander has slender, delicately branched stems, and thin, pointed taproots with few branches.
- Produces lacy clusters of tiny white, pink, or purple flowers about 2 or 3 months after sowing.
- Small, round, ribbed seeds, which follow the flowers, have a sweet, spicy aroma with a peppery, balsamic overtone, and a mildly burning taste with just a hint of orange peel. The aroma and taste of the mature dried seeds are quite different to that of the leaves, although fresh young seeds may have an odor that some would call unpleasant.
- Seeds, leaves, and roots may all be eaten.

CULTIVATION NOTES

- Coriander thrives in well-drained, fertile, deep, medium to heavy soil. Don't overfertilize, as too much nitrogen delays the ripening of the fruits (seeds) and diminishes their flavor. Tolerated pH range is 4.9 to 8.2.
- Tolerates cold and heat, but does require full sunlight and watering during dry periods.
- Grow coriander in a location that is protected from the wind, as the plants are susceptible to being blown over when they are top-heavy with seeds.

66

- Coriander does not transplant well, so sow seeds directly in the garden just after your last spring frost date. Plant seeds, with the husk left on, 6 mm (¼ inch) deep. Seedlings usually appear in 10 to 20 days.
- Thin seedlings 10 cm (4 inches) apart. Keep area free of weeds.
- Sow seeds every 3 weeks for a continuous supply of cilantro (leaves). The plants grow fast, and flower and go to seed quickly in hot weather. Leaf production stops once the plant flowers.

Paired seeds, sectioned above

- Generally pest-free, but susceptible to fungus diseases, especially in moist, rainy conditions and if the soil is too rich in nitrogen. Also liable to root rot, if the soil is poorly drained.
- Self-seeds readily, and if unchecked, can become a persistent weed.
- Coriander survives light frost very well, but is an annual that does not overwinter. However, as the plants often establish themselves from the dropped seeds of the previous season's crop, you can look forward to an early yield next year.

Coriander comes from the Greek word for "bug," koros, because the distinctive smell of the leaves is like that of bed bugs.

HARVESTING NOTES

- Pick leaves (cilantro) for fresh use as required when plants are 5 to 15 cm (2 to 6 inches) tall. Cilantro will keep for about 2 weeks in the refrigerator, especially if wrapped in a damp towel and enclosed in a plastic bag.
- Alternatively, set a cilantro plant in a bottle of water, making sure the leaves are tightly enclosed in a plastic bag. Snip leaves as required.
- Although the leaves can be frozen in ice cubes, or hung to dry, the flavor is not as pronounced as when cilantro is used fresh.
- Harvest coriander seeds as soon as the fruit is light brown. Cut the stems at the base of the plant and put in a paper bag in a warm, dark location to dry. Shake the dried fruits in the bag to remove them from the stems, then rub the dried fruits between the palms of your hands to split them into seed segments. Store the seeds in an airtight container.
- Wash dug-up roots and freeze them for later use. Don't harvest the roots of flowering or fruiting plants, as they are inferior to those of young plants.

According to Chinese custom, eating coriander seeds helps one to attain immortality.

CULINARY USES

- Add fresh, tender, young cilantro to salads, and use as a garnish for fish and soups. Cilantro is an essential ingredient of salsa, tomato sauces, and chutneys, and is a staple in Asian, Mexican, South and Central American, and East Indian cuisine.
- Try cilantro in your favorite recipes for tuna, crab, salmon, snapper, and shrimp, and enjoy its special piquancy in stir-fry dishes and lamb stews, or with pork, cooked beans, fried

rice, and poultry. Cilantro loses its flavor quickly when cooked, so add it just prior to serving.
- Coriander seeds are a vital ingredient of curry powder, and all East Indian curry recipes. In India, the seeds are often lightly toasted before grinding to heighten their curry-like flavor. In Middle Eastern cooking, coriander is widely used in meat dishes and stews.
- Use coriander seeds, either whole or ground, in pickles, soups, sauces, fruit desserts, such as stewed apples or prunes, and with all types of meat dishes. Add to mulled wine to impart a warm, summery flavor.
- Ground coriander is used commercially to flavor baked goods and processed meats such as hot dogs and sausages, while the oil extracted from the seeds is used in the preparation of canned soups, sauces, candy, chewing gum, ice cream, liqueurs, gin, and even tobacco products.
- Boil the roots, Thai-style, to flavor soups and chicken dishes.

CRAFT USES
- Include fragrant coriander seeds in potpourris and sachets.

Early Sanskrit writings indicate that coriander was known as far back as 5000 BC. It is said to have added fragrance to the Hanging Gardens of Babylon, one of the Seven Wonders of the Ancient World.

MEDICINAL USES
- In Asian folk medicine, coriander has been used to treat stomach problems, nausea, fevers, measles, colds, and hernias. In Western folk medicine, coriander was used primarily for digestive and gastric complaints.
- Coriander is not used in modern Western medicine.
- Coriander seed oil is used in the pharmaceutical industry to mask the unpleasant taste of various medicines.
- Cilantro is rich in minerals and vitamins A, B, and C. Because it contains next to no calories, it's a favorite herb of dieters.

CAUTIONS
- Some people may experience dermatitis after handling the leaves of coriander or from coming in contact with the oil from the seeds.

Queen Elizabeth I (1533–1603) is said to have loved hard candies made with coriander seeds.

CRESS
Cruciferae (Brassicaceae; mustard family)

GARDEN CRESS
Lepidium sativum

Also known as: Common garden cress, curled cress, land cress, pepper cress, pepper grass, pepperwort.

UPLAND CRESS
Barbarea verna

Also known as: American cress, American winter cress, bank cress, Belle Isle cress, early winter cress, herb of St. Barbara, Normandy cress, spring cress, treacle mustard, wormseed

DESCRIPTION

- Garden cress, a native of western Asia, the Near East, and Ethiopia, is a fast-growing annual. A favorite English salad herb since the 16th century, garden cress grows from 20 to 80 cm (8 to 32 inches) tall. Upland cress, a native of Europe and another old salad crop, is a biennial (sometimes perennial) herbaceous plant. Depending on environmental condition, upland cress flowering stalks grow from 30 to 90 cm (12 to 36 inches) tall.
- The most popular garden cress has lacy leaves that resemble curled parsley, but the foliage is lighter and more delicate. Non-curled forms of garden cress, with broader leaves, are also available. Upland cress has shiny, lobed leaves. Cress leaves have a pleasantly spicy, peppery taste, reminiscent of watercress, only more pungent.
- Garden cress and upland cress resemble dandelions in that each first produces a rosette, which is a very short stem that bears crowded leaves radiating outward in a flattish circle. The plant then sends up a flowering stem. Both cresses have branching taproots.
- Garden cress produces small, white (sometimes red), fragrant, peppery-tasting flowers, while upland cress flowers are yellow. Both cresses bloom in late spring and beyond, if sown later in the season.
- Garden cress is more popular and easier to grow than upland cress, and may also be grown indoors for winter use.
- Leaves, sprouts, and young flower buds of both cresses may be eaten.

CULTIVATION NOTES

- Cresses grow best in moist, rich, well-drained soil or well-rotted compost. Tolerated pH range for garden cress is 4.9 to 8.0; for upland cress the pH range is 4.5 to 7.5.

Garden cress in flower

*D*ILL *Anethum graveolens*
Umbelliferae (Apiaceae; carrot family)
Also known as: American dill, common dill, Danish dill, dill seed, dilly, European dill, garden dill

DESCRIPTION

- Dill, which originated in southwestern Asia, is a striking, hardy annual that grows from 30 to 120 cm (1 to 4 feet) tall.
- Thread-like, shiny, bluish-green leaves have a distinctive slightly sharp, spicy, persistent flavor and aroma.
- Dill has cylindrical, thin, hollow stems, and a slender, spindle-like taproot with few branches. The root can be anywhere from 10 to 30 cm (4 to 12 inches) long.
- Produces umbrella-like clusters of numerous tiny yellowish flowers from July to September. Clusters may be up to 8 cm (about 3 inches) wide.
- Seeds, which follow the flowers, are flat, ribbed, and very numerous. Dill seeds have a warm, pungent, sharp, tangy flavor, and a fragrance that resembles caraway.
- May be grown indoors for winter use.
- Leaves, seed heads, and seeds may all be eaten.

CULTIVATION NOTES

- Dill is tolerant of organic soils, but it grows best in deep, well-drained, fertile, sandy loam that is supplemented with compost or manure. Recommended pH range is 5.5 to 6.5.
- Must be grown in full sunlight. Requires watering during dry periods.
- When the hollow stalks are top-heavy with seeds they are susceptible to being knocked over by the wind, so it's best to plant dill in a protected location.
- As dill prefers cooler temperatures, you can plant seeds directly in the garden early in the spring, when night temperatures are as low as -4°C (25°F). Sow seeds 6 mm (¼ inch) deep,

where you want the plants to grow. (Dill doesn't transplant well as the long taproot is easily damaged.) Seeds usually germinate within 2 weeks. Young plants are very tolerant of late spring frosts.

- Thin plants 15 cm (6 inches) apart.
- Make a second planting in July to ensure a continuous supply of fresh leaves throughout the growing season.
- Hot weather causes dill to flower, which reduces leaf production.
- Generally pest- and disease-free. To prevent mildew developing on the seed heads, avoid overhead sprinkling when plants are more than 60 cm (2 feet) high.
- Dill self-sows readily. Seeds can overwinter outdoors up to zone 3, germinating in the garden the following year.
- Indoor plants require at least 5 hours of direct sunlight or 12 hours of bright artificial light daily. Apply a high nitrate fertilizer. To limit damage to indoor plants, trim no more than 10 cm (4 inches) from the stems at any one time. For good re-growth, leave at least 10 cm (4 inches) of stem at the base. Indoor dill plants have a useful life of about 3 months.

The name "dill" comes from the Old Norse dilla meaning "to lull," a reference to the herb's soothing effect on crying babies.

HARVESTING NOTES

- Start harvesting leaves before flowering begins, when plants are about 15 cm (6 inches) tall. Harvest from summer through early fall.
- For best flavor, use the leaves fresh. Cut them in the morning, when the dew has dried.
- Freezing preserves dill's flavor well. Simply freeze the leaves in an air-tight container.
- To dry dill, cut whole stems with foliage and hang them upside down. When dry, strip the leaves from the stems, and store in an airtight container.
- Collect seed heads for pickles as soon as the flowers are fully open, but before the seeds ripen. Cut off seed heads, with a small portion of stem attached, and enclose in a paper bag. When the seed heads turn brown, remove from the bag, and store in an airtight container.
- To obtain dried seeds, harvest ripe seed heads along with a small portion of the accompanying stem. Enclose seed heads in a paper bag. Hang the enclosed seed heads upside down by the stems to dry in a cool, airy location. Store dried seeds in an airtight container.

The ancient Romans believed dill had fortifying properties, so they applied it liberally to food given to gladiators.

> *Early American colonists used to eat dill seed to help ward off hunger during the long hours they spent in church. Over time, the seeds became known as "meeting seeds."*

CULINARY USES

- Dill leaves, seed heads, and seeds are essential for flavoring and seasoning pickled vegetables such as cucumbers.
- Add finely chopped fresh leaves or dried dill to seafood dishes, particularly salmon, soups, salads and salad dressing, poultry, eggs, meats, stews, casseroles, vegetables, especially peas and beans and members of the cabbage family, herb butter, sour cream, sauces, cream cheese, and dips.
- When cooking with fresh dill, add it at the last minute for maximum flavor and aroma.
- Add fresh leaves to vinegar and extra-virgin olive oil.

> *In the Middle Ages, dill was said to protect against witchcraft. It was also a key ingredient of exotic love potions and aphrodisiacs.*

CRAFT USES

- Include dill's yellow flower clusters in fresh floral bouquets.

MEDICINAL USES

- Dill was once widely used for treating stomach ache, colic, hiccups, bad breath, flatulence, and hemorrhoids. It is still employed for such purposes in various parts of the world. As there is no proof of the medical effectiveness of dill, it's not used in modern Western medicine.
- Dill is rich in vitamin C, which explains why it was once used to treat scurvy.

> *Flemish and German brides have traditionally carried dill or worn sprigs of it on their wedding gowns to ensure a happy marriage.*

CAUTIONS

- Some people may experience dermatitis after contact with dill.
- Dill may cause some individuals to experience photodermatitis, a skin rash that appears after eating the herb and subsequently being exposed to sunlight.

CULTIVARS AND RELATIVES

- Indian dill (*A. graveolens* subsp. *sowa*). Pungent, somewhat bitter seeds are an essential ingredient of curry powder.

> *A mixture of dill, dried honey, and butter was once a standard prescription for treating madness.*

FENNEL *Foeniculum vulgare*
Umbelliferae (Apiaceae; carrot family)
Also known as: Common fennel, Roman fennel.

DESCRIPTION

- Fennel, a southern European and Mediterranean native, is a graceful perennial that is grown as an annual in most parts of northern North America. This handsome herb, which grows from 0.6 to 1.5 m (2 to 5 feet) tall, was brought to North America by Spanish priests, and may still be found growing wild around old missions.
- Soft, blue-green, feathery leaves, which are similar to those of dill, are dissected into fine, thread-like segments. The foliage has an elusive flavor and aroma that is reminiscent of aniseed and parsley.
- Fennel has erect, solid, pithy, many-branched stems, and a large, spindle-shaped root.
- Produces clusters of tiny yellow flowers in mid- to late summer.
- Egg-shaped, ribbed seeds, which follow the flowers, have a stronger aniseed fragrance and taste than the foliage.
- Both leaves and seeds are edible.

CULTIVATION NOTES

- Fennel grows well in almost any good soil, but it performs best in deep, well-drained, non-acidic soil. Tolerated pH range is 4.8 to 8.2.
- Prefers full sunlight, but will grow in light shade. Fennel needs to be protected from the wind, so you will need to stake it, or cultivate it near a fence or wall. Requires watering during dry spells, and is inclined to bolt when the temperature climbs.
- Sow seeds directly in the garden as soon as the ground can be worked, usually a couple of weeks before your last spring frost date. (Sow seeds where you want the plants to grow, as fennel does not transplant easily.) Soil temperature is best between 15° and 18°C (60° and 65°F).
- Plant seeds 0.6 to 1 cm (¼ to ½ inch) deep. Seedlings usually emerge in 10 to 14 days. Thin plants to 20 cm (8 inches) apart.

- Can also be propagated by dividing established plants in the spring. Space the divisions 30 cm (12 inches) apart.
- Do not grow near dill, as fennel and dill can cross-pollinate. This is unlikely to change the taste of the seeds that are produced, but the hybrid seeds can't be used to grow either good fennel or good dill.
- Cut back some stems throughout the growing season to ensure an ongoing supply of new stems and leaves.
- Susceptible to infestations of white fly and aphids, and to root rot if the soil is too moist.
- While fennel has been known to overwinter outdoors in a protected location up to zone 5, it is generally grown as an annual in short-season gardens because it is susceptible to freezing.

The ancient Chinese used fennel as a remedy for snakebite, while early Greek athletes training for the Olympic Games ate the seeds to help control their weight.

HARVESTING NOTES

- Pick leaves for fresh use throughout the summer right up to frost. Collect the leaves in the morning, after the dew has evaporated.
- To dry fennel, harvest stems with leaves before the plants flower and hang upside down to air-dry in a cool location. When dry, strip leaves and store in an airtight container.
- Freeze leaves in ice cubes.
- Harvest the mature seed heads in the fall, when they ripen. Spread the gray-green seeds in a thin layer on a screen in the shade to dry, turning them often. Store dried seeds in an airtight container.

The famous Battle of Marathon, in 490 BC, which celebrates the routing of a Persian army by a much smaller Greek force, was fought on a field of fennel. Statues of Pheidippides, the Athenian athlete who ran 240 km (150 miles) to Sparta to summons help against the Persians, always show him holding a sprig of fennel. Indeed, the Greek word marathon *means "fennel."*

CULINARY USES

- Use finely chopped fennel leaves and stems in stuffing, marinades, sauces for vegetables, and in herbed butter and cheese spreads. Fennel goes particularly well in tomato and cucumber salads, and makes a tasty garnish for asparagus.
- Add leaves to your favorite fish recipes, especially those calling for oily, strongly flavored fish, such as mackerel. Fennel will help offset the odor and promote digestion. Stuff the fish with fresh leaves, or add leaves to the water for poached fish. Fennel is essential for the classic Provençal dish *Grillade au Fenouil*, in which grilled sea bass, red mullet, or trout is flamed in brandy on a bed of dried fennel stalks.
- Add fresh leaves to hot dishes just before serving, as heat quickly reduces the flavor of the leaves.

- Use the stronger-flavored seeds in stews, sausages, pickles, sauerkraut, beans and lentils, salad dressing, tomato-based sauces, breads, cookies, and cakes.
- Fennel seeds are used commercially in condiments, ice cream, prepared meats such as pepperoni, and liqueurs, especially anisette.
- Add fresh leaves to extra-virgin olive oil or other cooking oil.

Fennel is occasionally the host for the so-called parsley worm, a rather impressive caterpillar that is tiger-striped green, cream, and black with orange spots. The parsley worm is the larval stage of the beautiful swallowtail butterfly, Papilio.

CRAFT USES
- Include fennel's dainty yellow flowers in fresh summer floral bouquets.

MEDICINAL USES
- Infusions of fennel leaves or decoctions of seeds were used in traditional herbal medicine to stimulate the appetite and relieve flatulence and abdominal cramps in adults and children. Fennel water is an old folk remedy for reducing infant colic. Eating a few fennel seeds before a meal was recommended to help curb the appetite, while chewing seeds after a meal was said to aid digestion. Modern research has proven the value of all these traditional uses.
- Another old medicinal use of fennel that has persisted to the present is the treatment of infections of the upper respiratory tract. Indeed, there is evidence that fennel has the capacity to counteract inflammation, microbial infections, and the spasms associated with lung diseases.
- Fennel has an ancient reputation for affecting the female reproductive cycle, supposedly promoting menstruation, increasing milk supply, relieving menopausal symptoms, and even strengthening libido. Estrogen-like substances have been found to occur in fennel, suggesting that these observations may be valid. Research is ongoing in this area.
- Fennel is widely used in the pharmaceutical industry to mask the unpleasant taste of many medicines.
- Fennel leaves contain thiamine, riboflavin, niacin, ascorbic acid, and some ß-carotene, and protein. The seeds contain iodine and vitamin A.

Legend has it that female deer purge themselves with fennel before giving birth.

CAUTIONS

- The oil found in fennel can cause contact dermatitis in some people, although allergic skin reactions to the herb are rare.
- Fennel may also cause some individuals to experience photodermatitis, a rash that appears after eating the herb and subsequently being exposed to sunlight.
- Because fennel oil has also been known to cause nausea, vomiting, seizures, and pulmonary edema, you should never use it in preparing food. However, the foliage and seeds are safe.
- Given the potential estrogenic effect of fennel, you should not consume large amounts of the herb if you are pregnant.
- Diabetics must consider the sugar content of commercial preparations of fennel syrup and fennel honey.

CULTIVARS AND RELATIVES

- Florence fennel or finocchio (*F. vulgare* var. *azoricum*). Develops an edible, swollen, leaf base, or bulb, rather similar to that of celery. Delicate anise flavor. Because of its aroma, Florence fennel is often mistakenly marketed as anise. All parts are edible, including the basal stalks, which can be eaten raw in salads, or served as a cooked vegetable, ideally roasted. Cultivated as an annual, Florence fennel is not a true herb, although it is sometimes treated as such in nursery catalogs.
- Bronze fennel (*F. vulgare* var. *dulce* 'Bronze'). Bronze-red, lacy foliage adds interest and color to any herb garden. Substitute leaves for green fennel in salads and fish dishes. Bronze fennel is more winter-hardy than most varieties.

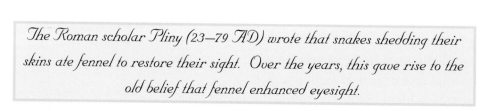

The Roman scholar Pliny (23–79 AD) wrote that snakes shedding their skins ate fennel to restore their sight. Over the years, this gave rise to the old belief that fennel enhanced eyesight.

_F_ENUGREEK _Trigonella foenum-graecum_

Leguminosae (Fabaceae; pea family)

Also known as: Billy-goat clover, billy-goat hay, camel grass, common fenugreek, fenugrec, Greek clover, Greek hayseed

Annual

DESCRIPTION

- Fenugreek is a spicy, aromatic, hardy annual that grows from 30 to 60 cm (1 to 2 feet) tall. This ancient culinary and medicinal plant is known from an archaeological site in Iraq that has been dated at 4000 BC.
- Bright green leaves have 3 oval-shaped, toothed leaflets, much like clover. Although young leaves typically have a bitterish taste, the plant has a strong sweet-clover scent, reminiscent of vanilla.
- Fenugreek has fairly stiff, hollow stems that are branched at the bases, and a long taproot that has numerous fine laterals with nitrogen-fixing nodules.
- Produces small, scented flowers that are usually pale yellow, sometimes white, and occasionally tinged with lilac at the base. Flowers grow singly or in pairs. Plants bloom in late summer.
- Long, narrow, curved seed pods that follow the flowers are green or reddish before ripening, and straw-colored or light brown at maturity. Each pod contains from 10 to 20 oblong, olive green seeds, about 6 mm (¼ inch) long, with tiny bumps. Fresh seeds taste and smell somewhat like lovage and celery. Ground seed has a very distinctive maple-sweet yet spicy, mildly bitter flavor. The aroma, while comparable to that of burnt sugar, is highly appetizing.
- Both seeds and leaves are edible.

CULTIVATION NOTES

- Fenugreek requires well-drained, good soil of medium texture. Tolerated pH range is 5.3 to 8.2.
- Bacterial nodules on the roots take up nitrogen from the air, so this leguminous plant needs little if any nitrogen fertilizer, and actually enriches the soil with nitrogen.
- Needs full sunlight, and requires watering during dry periods.

- While fenugreek is easy to grow, most available cultivars need a growing season of 4 to 5 months, although some cultivars mature seeds just 3 months after sowing. It's a short-day plant, with flowering only beginning as the days shorten in late summer.
- Sow seed directly in the garden in spring, as soon as the danger of frost is past.
- Plant seeds 6 mm (¼ inch) deep. Germination takes place 7 to 10 days after sowing.
- Space plants 10 cm (4 inches) apart.
- Sow seeds every 3 weeks for a regular supply of young plants for use in salads.
- Usually pest-free, but susceptible to Cercospora leaf spot, a fungus disease.

> *The generic name Trigonella comes from the Greek treis, meaning "three," and gonu, meaning "angle" or "corner," a reference to the triangular appearance of the flowers of some of the species. The specific epithet foenum-graecum is Latin for "Greek hay," and refers to the longstanding Greek practice of using the plant to scent and fortify hay.*

HARVESTING NOTES

- Pick whole plants for fresh use in salads when they are about 5 cm (2 inches) high (cut off the roots).
- After the seeds have matured, uproot the plants and hang to dry. When seeds are completely dry, thresh and separate them. Grind seeds if required. Store whole dried seeds or ground fenugreek powder in airtight containers.

CULINARY USES

- Add freshly chopped young leaves to salads, vegetable bean soups, stews, and cauliflower and potato dishes. Use sparingly, as the leaves are rather bitter.
- Use ground fenugreek seeds in your favorite curry dishes. Ground seeds are an essential ingredient of curry powders, oriental sauces, and spice mixtures, and halvah, the delicious Jewish sweetmeat.
- Flavor pickles, chutneys, especially mango, with fenugreek seeds, either ground or whole.
- Sprout the seeds to add to salads or sandwiches. Simply cover the bottom of a container with a thin layer of seeds. Rinse seeds, and leave overnight in a bowl of cold water. In the morning, put the seeds in a plastic container and place it in a warm, dark spot. Rinse the sprouts twice a day to keep them fresh. After each rinse, return the container to its warm location. You should have fresh sprouts ready for eating in about 4 days. (If you notice any fungus growing on the seeds or sprouts, discard them.)
- Fenugreek seeds or extracts are used commercially to flavor pickles, baked goods, candy, condiments, chewing gum, soft drinks, gelatins, pudding, ice cream, icing, and syrups, such as maple, caramel, butterscotch, and vanilla.
- In India, roasted seeds are used as a coffee substitute.

> *Since ancient times, fenugreek has been fed to livestock. It is added to hay of inferior quality to make it more palatable, and it is used as a stimulant and appetizer in livestock food and tonic preparations.*

During the four-year Roman siege of Jerusalem, which began in AD 66, the city's Jewish defenders added fenugreek to the boiling oil and water that they poured on the Roman troops as they climbed ladders to scale the city walls. As ground fenugreek mixed with water becomes glutinous and slippery, many a Roman must have lost his footing and tumbled to the ground below.

MEDICINAL USES

- Fenugreek is one of the oldest medicinal plants, and has been used in folk medicine for a wide variety of uses, most of which have not been medically validated. It is clear, however, that fenugreek has medicinal properties. It reduces blood sugar and increases milk flow, and it can be applied to the skin to reduce irritations. Because medical use for any of these purposes can have undesirable side effects, you should not attempt self-medication.
- In modern European herbal medicine, fenugreek is sometimes used as a mild laxative, as an expectorant for people suffering from bronchitis and sore throats, and as a nutritive tea for convalescents. It is also used to treat stomach problems.
- In modern medicine, fenugreek seeds, which contain diosgenin, are used in the synthesis of oral contraceptives and sex hormones, as well as other pharmaceutical products. Diosgenin (from several plant sources) is the starting compound for over 60 percent of all manufactured steroids.
- Fenugreek seeds contain protein, oil, and carbohydrate, and are considered to be quite nutritious. The fresh plant is a good source of protein, vitamins B and C, and potassium.
- Fenugreek is used in modern veterinary medicine in the treatment of livestock, particularly horses. It also seems to stimulate milk production in dairy cattle.

In ancient Egypt, fenugreek was used in making kuphi, *the holy smoke or incense used in fumigation and embalming.*

CAUTIONS

- Because of fenugreek's estrogen content and its ability to stimulate the uterus, you should avoid this herb if you are pregnant.
- Fenugreek lowers blood sugar levels, and has been used experimentally as an oral insulin substitute. If you are diabetic, you should be aware that consuming fenugreek might interfere with your insulin therapy.
- As some authorities suggest that fenugreek's high mucilage content could coat the stomach and reduce absorption of prescription drugs, you should limit your consumption of fenugreek if you are taking medication.

Until recently, women in Libya and Eritrea ate fenugreek seeds to gain weight. In some countries in Africa and the Middle East, the seeds have long had a reputation for promoting fuller, more rounded breasts.

GARLIC *Allium sativum*
Liliaceae (lily family)
Also known as: Heal-all, rustic's treacle, poor man's treacle, stinking rose

DESCRIPTION

- Garlic, for thousands of years a culinary and medical standby in many parts of the world, is a moderately hardy, herbaceous perennial that grows from 0.6 to 1 m (2 to 3 feet) tall. It is thought to have originated from wild garlic, perhaps in the desert of Kirghiz in western Asia.
- Several flat, green leaves extend from the base and encase the lower stem. Young leaves have a delicate chive-like aroma and taste. Leaves can reach up to 0.6 m (2 feet) in height.
- Erect, hollow, green stalks support small, pink or whitish flowering clusters, or bulbils, which appear in midsummer. Bulbils have a mild garlic flavor. Flowering stalks may be as much as 1 m (3 feet) tall.
- Bulb is made up of swollen, modified leaves, like that of an onion. Unlike an onion, a garlic bulb's leaves are organized into segments called cloves. There may be anywhere from 4 to 15 cloves in a bulb. Cloves are joined to the central axis of the plant, and are often encased in a papery sheath, which can range in color from pink to tan.
- Leaves, bulbs, and bulbils may all be eaten.

CULTIVATION NOTES

- Garlic does best in rich, well-drained, highly organic soils, although it will grow in a wide range of soils. Tolerated pH range is 5.5 to 8.5.
- Prefers full sun, but will grow in partial shade. Avoid overwatering or the bulbs will rot.
- As garden garlic does not produce seeds, grow it from cloves or bulbils, which are available from nurseries and through garden catalogs.
- Cloves can be planted in early spring or late fall; however, fall plantings produce the best yields, as garlic needs a rather long growing season (at least 4 months). If you plant in late September or October, you can expect to see tops showing above the soil by November,

and the plants will be well rooted. Cloves or young plants are dormant over the winter, resuming growth when the snow melts in the spring. During dormancy, cloves or young plants need exposure to cold temperatures between 0° C and 10° C (32°F and 50°F) for 4 to 8 weeks in order to form new bulbs. Increasing daylight in the spring not only helps break the plant's dormancy, but also stimulates bulbing.

- Plant cloves, with the pointed end up, 5 cm (2 inches) below the soil's surface. (If overwintering plants in zones 3 and 4, plant cloves at least 8 cm (3 inches) deep.) Cloves need space, so leave an area about 15 cm (6 inches) around each one.
- As garlic is shallow-rooted, do not cultivate too deeply or you will damage the roots and retard the plant's growth.
- Cut back the flowering stalks in midsummer to help channel the plant's energy into the developing bulbs.
- Generally pest- and disease-free.
- Overwinters outdoors up to zone 3. In the northernmost range, especially where snow cover is limited, mulch the cloves or young plants over the winter.

> *The genus name Allium is thought to come from the Celtic all, meaning "pungent." The word "garlic" is derived from the Anglo-Saxon gar, meaning "lance" (after the shape of the stem) and leac, meaning "pot-herb."*

HARVESTING NOTES

- Harvest garlic when the tops dry out and begin to collapse.
- Pull up the mature plants with their large, multi-clove bulbs and dry them in the sun for a week. Then trim or braid the stalks and hang the garlic "ropes" in the shade to dry further.
- Store in a cool, dry, airy, dark place. Try not to keep garlic in the kitchen as the heat dries out the bulbs. If you must have a plentiful garlic supply within easy reach while you're cooking, keep the bulbs in a closed jar so the pungent odor doesn't penetrate nearby foods.
- Garlic can keep for up to 6 months in a dry, dark location, providing the temperature is no higher than 0°C (32°F).

> *During World War I, garlic was widely used to combat typhus and dysentery, and to disinfect wounds. Raw garlic juice was diluted with water and put on swabs of sterilized sphagnum moss, which was then applied to battle wounds to prevent septic poisoning or gangrene. By World War II, antibiotics, especially penicillin, had replaced garlic for these uses. The Red Army, however, was so short of antibiotics that Russian doctors had to rely heavily on garlic once again.*
>
> *As a result, garlic came to be called Russian penicillin.*

CULINARY USES

- Use garlic, fresh, dried, or powdered—fresh is best—to enhance the flavor of seafood, poultry, pasta, meat dishes, stews, casseroles, vegetables, and soups, and to add zest to salads and salad dressings. Garlic is the essential ingredient in *ailloli*, the hearty, thick French mayonnaise made with eggs, olive oil, and crushed garlic. And what is a plate of pasta without hot, crispy garlic bread?

- Use a garlic press or mortar and pestle to crush fresh cloves or hit the cloves sharply with the flat end of a knife blade. Just how much garlic to add to a recipe is always contentious—use sparingly until you've established the garlic tolerance zone of the diners.
- Steam or bake whole cloves. Garlic's flavor becomes milder with cooking; however, burnt garlic just tastes bitter. When frying garlic, make sure the oil is not too hot, as the garlic will develop an acrid taste.
- Prevent the skin of fresh garlic from sticking to your fingers when you're peeling it by dropping the cloves in boiling water for 30 seconds. Remove, drain, cool, and peel.
- Garlic salt is widely used commercially to flavor foods. It's also a popular standby in home kitchens, although its high sodium content makes it an unwise flavoring choice in healthy heart cooking.

The ancient Egyptians were probably garlic's greatest fans. Known as the "stinking ones" because of their garlic breath, the Egyptians swore sacred oaths on garlic and used the herb like money. Pharaohs were entombed with carvings of garlic and onions to ensure an afterlife replete with well-seasoned meals. An ancient Egyptian papyrus dated at 1600 BC recounts a strike among the men working on the pyramids because their daily food ration did not include enough garlic. And the Bible tells us that after Moses led the Hebrew slaves out of Egypt, they began to grumble about their harsh life in the wilderness and complained about missing such niceties as garlic.

MEDICINAL USES
- Garlic has been used for centuries in folk medicine to treat everything from abscesses, boils, cancer, diarrhea, diphtheria, typhoid, and hepatitis to heart problems, hypertension, blood clots, gangrene, plague, cholera, typhus, meningitis, dysentery, and intestinal worms.
- In modern herbal medicine, eating at least 5 cloves of fresh garlic daily is said to contribute to good health; however, this level of consumption may cause heartburn, flatulence, and other gastrointestinal problems, to say nothing of social ostracism.
- In modern medicine, garlic is being studied for its antibiotic potential and its effectiveness in helping to prevent heart and stroke disease and some tumors. Garlic may also prove to be useful for diabetics, as it seems to help regulate blood sugar levels. For medicinal purposes, fresh garlic is vastly superior to dried garlic.

Garlic was considered to be a defense against vampires, a belief said to have been disseminated widely by that most famous of all vampires, Count Dracula. Since garlic is a blood-thinner, the Count could feast more readily on those who had consumed it.

CAUTIONS

- Some people may experience dermatitis from garlic dust.
- Garlic consumption reduces blood-clotting time, which can cause medical problems for people taking aspirin or other anticoagulant drugs.
- If you are diabetic, you should be aware that if you take garlic in medicinal quantities, for example, garlic pills, it can interfere with your insulin therapy.
- If you suffer from any medical problem that requires medication, you should consult your doctor before consuming garlic extracts.
- Although garlic consumption is generally safe, some authorities have recommended against consuming too much garlic if you are pregnant or breast-feeding.

While it may be true that garlic breath is only a problem for non-garlic eaters, many remedies for this anti-social state have been tried over the years. Chewing parsley remains the most popular, but other remedies include chewing coffee beans, cloves, cardamom seeds, chervil, and mint-flavored chewing gum. The French favor drinking red wine, but probably the most effective method is to rinse the mouth and clean the teeth with chloramine. As garlic's odor is also eliminated via the skin, the sensitive should be resigned to the occasional odoriferous transit journey or crowd experience, especially in warm weather.

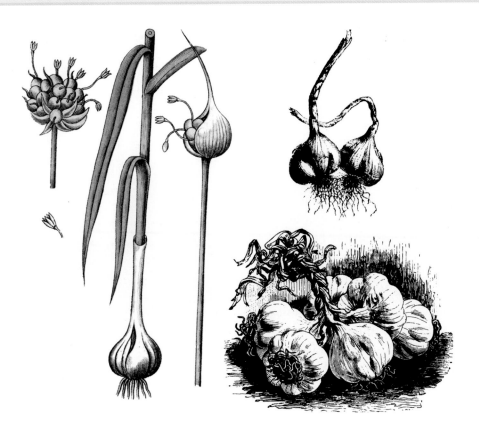

*G*ERANIUMS, SCENTED   *Pelargonium* species

Geraniaceae (geranium family)

Also known as: Pelargonium, stork's bill, sweet-scented geranium

DESCRIPTION

- Scented geraniums come in a wide range of shapes, sizes, scents, and colors. Depending on species or cultivar, these fragrant perennials, which are cultivated as annuals in northern gardens, can smell like apple and cinnamon, roses, mint, camphor, lemons, nutmeg, pineapples, limes, oranges, or coconut. Native mainly to South Africa, scented geraniums grow from about 0.3 to 1 m (1 to 3 feet) tall.

- Leaves vary greatly in shape, size, and texture, depending on the species or cultivar. Some are deeply cut like oak leaves, others are finely cut like ferns. Still others are crinkled or curled like parsley. Scented geranium leaves can be dainty or robust, sticky or furry. Some are light green, some are dark green, some are grayish-green, and all have their own distinctive flavor and scent.

- Scented geraniums produce flowers in open clusters. The flowers, which are not as showy as those of standard garden geraniums, range from pale pink or white through lavender and cerise. The lower 3 petals of the flowers are smaller than the upper 2 petals, which are often attractively streaked with a deeper color.

- May be grown in pots and containers, both outside and indoors.

- Both flowers and leaves may be eaten.

CULTIVATION NOTES

- Scented geraniums thrive in well-rotted, well-drained compost and fertile soils.
- Although scented geraniums grow and flower best under cool conditions and full sun, they can endure some drought, and indeed are likely to be damaged by heavy rains.

Peppermint geranium

- Most scented geraniums can be grown from seed, which can take anywhere from several weeks to several months to germinate. Sow seeds in a shallow flat, and keep on a heated mat. Do not let the temperature dip below 13°C (55°F). Transplant seedlings into small pots.
- Alternatively, and preferably, propagate from stem cuttings. Take cuttings in early fall, after the plants have flowered and before the threat of frost. Using a sharp knife, cut a stem just below a node, that is, where the leaf grows from the stem. Cuttings should be about 8 to 13 cm (3 to 5 inches) long. Remove all but 3 leaves. Dip the cut end in root-stimulating hormone, then insert the cutting in a mixture of sand and peat to root. After watering, place cuttings in the shade for a few days, then gradually expose them to sunlight. Thereafter, keep the cuttings on the dry side. Pot the cuttings when the roots are about 2 cm (¾ inch) long.
- Space garden plants 30 cm (12 inches) apart.
- Transplant potted cuttings to larger pots to keep pace with the plants' growth.
- Susceptible to root rot, bacterial wilt, and botrytis, and to infestations of whiteflies.
- Scented geraniums do not tolerate frost and must be wintered indoors in northern climates.
- Indoor plants need at least 4 hours of direct sunlight or 14 to 18 hours of artificial light daily. As the plants like to be fairly cool, place the pots close to a sunny but cool window. Water sparingly, allowing the soil to become barely dry between waterings. (Don't let the soil dry out completely, as the lower leaves will yellow and fall off.) Apply a half-strength houseplant fertilizer every 2 weeks during the flowering season, and monthly thereafter.
- To prevent indoor plants from growing too large and taking too much room, keep the roots slightly pot-bound. Prune the stem tips regularly to encourage branching. Infestations of whiteflies can weaken indoor plants, but they usually recover once taken outside again in the spring.

Pelargonium species were introduced to England from South Africa's Cape Province in 1632. Curiously, they don't grow best in their natural habitat because the South African spring, although ideal, lasts for only a few weeks, while the summer is far too hot. Summers in Europe, however, are just right, as tourists who have seen splendid beds of scented geraniums on their European travels will confirm.

HARVESTING NOTES

- Pick leaves for fresh use at any time after the plants are about 15 cm (6 inches) tall.
- Harvest leaves for drying before plants flower.
- Cut flower clusters for fresh use or for drying when most, but not all, of the blossoms have opened.
- Spread leaves and flowers on a cookie tray to dry in an airy, shaded location. Store dried flowers and crumbled leaves in an airtight container.

Pelargonium is derived from the Greek pelargos, meaning "a stork," because the fruit is long and slender like a stork's bill.

CULINARY USES

- Toss fresh flowers in green salads for a colorful, fragrant effect.
- Put a fresh scented geranium leaf in the bottom of the pan to enhance the flavor of angel food cake, butter cake, or sponge cake.
- To make a flavoring liquid from the leaves, infuse fresh or dried leaves in milk or water. Strain the liquid and use to flavor sauces, custards, jellies, sweet breads, ice creams and sherbets, jams, syrups, butter, and vinegar.
- Freeze sprigs of lemon or mint scented geranium in ice cubes and add to summer punches and iced tea.
- Brew a refreshing cup of tea by steeping 15 mL (3 teaspoons) of crushed fresh leaves or 5 mL (1 teaspoon) of dried leaves in 250 mL (1 cup) of boiling water. Lemon, rose, apricot, peach, orange, nutmeg, and coconut scented geraniums all make excellent herbal tea.

Pelargonium 'Citrosa' or 'Mosquito Fighter' is known for its citronella scent. Marketed a few years ago as Nature's original insect repellent, the plants were suddenly in great demand and short supply—and prices shot up accordingly. Although studies have since shown that 'Mosquito Fighter' has no effect on mosquitoes, black flies, or any other insect, it is still grown for its refreshing scent. The plant should be approached with care, as some people may experience nausea or burning eyes or shortness of breath simply from being near it. 'Mosquito Fighter' should never be eaten.

CRAFT USES

- Use freshly cut scented geranium flowers to make a fragrant table centerpiece.
- Include the aromatic dried leaves and flowers in potpourris and sachets.

MEDICINAL USES

- In traditional folk medicine, scented geranium was used to treat ulcers, headaches, and earaches. In some parts of Latin America, bathing in scented geranium water is said to help relieve skin irritations. In their native South Africa, *Pelargonium* species were used to treat diarrhea, dysentery, and syphilis.
- Scented geraniums are not used in modern Western medicine.
- Scented geranium oils are used commercially in perfumes, cosmetics, and soap.

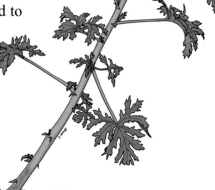

'Mosquito Fighter' geranium

CAUTIONS

- Some people may experience skin irritations from handling scented geraniums.

CULTIVARS AND RELATIVES

When selecting scented geraniums for culinary use, avoid those that lack an appetizing aroma, but note that a pleasing fragrance does not always guarantee a pleasing taste. There are about 300 species of *Pelargonium*. Here are some culinary favorites:

- Apple-scented (*P. odoratissimum*). Delicious apple and cinnamon aroma. Much beloved by Victorian gardeners.
- Apricot-scented (*P. scabrum* 'M. Ninon'). Dark shiny leaves set off beautiful deep rose blooms. Tantalizing apricot fragrance.
- Chocolate Mint (*P. quercifolium* 'Chocolate Mint'). A strong minty scent some think is reminiscent of chocolate.
- Cinnamon-scented (*P. crispum* 'Cinnamon'). Ideal for potting. Compact growth habit with small, crisped leaves. Combines lemon scent with the lingering warmth of cinnamon.
- Coconut-scented (*P. grossularioides*). Small dark leaves have distinctive coconut scent. Trailing habit makes it perfect for window boxes and hanging baskets.
- Lemon-scented (*P. crispum* 'Minor'). Stiff upright plant has pretty pinkish flowers, dainty crisped leaves, and a refreshing lemon scent.
- Lime-scented (*P. × nervosum*). Diminutive dark green leaves give off a pronounced true lime fragrance.
- Peppermint-scented (*P. tomentosum*). Large velvety leaves, white flowers, and trailing habit. Ideal for hanging baskets. Fresh mint aroma.
- Rose-scented (*P. graveolens, P. × asperum*). An old favorite, with deeply cut crinkly leaves, pink flowers, and strong rose fragrance.

Chocolate Mint geranium

In Victorian homes, pots of scented geraniums were strategically positioned where ladies would be sure to brush the plants with their long skirts as they passed, thereby spreading the fragrant scents throughout the room.

In 1882, while sick in bed, Charles Darwin (1809–1882), entertained himself by studying a hop plant growing over his windowsill. The great student of evolution noted that the tip of the stem completed a revolution in 2 hours.

CULINARY USES

- Serve young hop shoots as you would asparagus. The shoots, which are best when they are 5 to 10 cm (2 to 4 inches) long, should be boiled for 2 to 3 minutes. Then change the water and steam the spears until tender. Serve with melted butter or cheese sauce. In hop-producing areas of Europe, blanched hop spears are sometimes served as a delicacy.
- Hops are an essential ingredient of beer, whether brewed at home or in commercial breweries, as it is the resin in the cones' lupulin glands that gives beer its bitterness.
- Hop extracts and oil are used commercially to flavor yeast, candy, ice cream, puddings, gelatins, baked goods, chewing gum, confectionery, and condiments.

Before yeast cakes became widely available in stores, yeast for making bread was prepared by culturing wild yeast in a decoction of hops and water. Some of this mixture was then added to the bread dough. The hops helped to flavor the bread and prevent the yeast from spoiling.

CRAFT USES

- Include the dried cones in wreaths and garlands.

MEDICINAL USES

- Hops were used for centuries to treat insomnia and a wide variety of ailments. Hops contain a tranquilizing alcohol, so although they are not used today in prescription medications, they are widely incorporated in over-the-counter commercial herbal relaxants.
- In modern European herbal medicine, hops continue to be used for some stomach problems, as their bitterness stimulates the appetite and increases the secretion of gastric juices.

The 9th century Arabian physician, Mesue, recommended the use of hops to induce sleep. Native North Americans have also traditionally used hops for their sedative properties.

CAUTIONS

- Individuals suffering from depression may want to avoid hops as the herb's sedative effect may actually accentuate the symptoms of this condition.
- The small grappling hooks that hop stems use to anchor to a trellis on which they climb can irritate the skin, so wear gloves when removing the dead vines in the fall.
- As hops have an anti-contractive effect, you should avoid consuming excessive amounts of this herb if you are pregnant.

HORSERADISH *Armoracia rusticana*
Cruciferae (Brassicaceae; mustard family)
Also known as: German mustard, redcole, stingnose

DESCRIPTION

- Horseradish, a stout, hardy, erect perennial that grows from 60 to 125 cm (2 to 4 feet) high, is believed to have originated in southern Russia. A handsome but highly invasive plant, horseradish is best reserved for a spot in your garden where it will not overshadow or crowd less resilient neighbors.
- Rather coarse, dark green leaves, commonly with crinkled edges, but with smooth edges in some cultivars. Young leaves have a pleasant, mildly spicy flavor.
- Horseradish has a stout, perennial, hard-fleshy taproot, about 30 cm (12 inches) long and 1 cm (½ inch) thick, with smaller roots branching from it. The taproot is corky-tan on the outside and white on the inside. The roots can reach as far as 5 m (16 feet) below the soil surface. Bruised roots give off a stronger, more powerful odor than that of freshly cut onions. The flavor of fresh horseradish root is hot, biting, and pungent.

- Produces flowering stems with small, aromatic, white blooms throughout the summer.
- Both roots and young spring leaves are edible.

CULTIVATION NOTES

- Horseradish grows in almost any soil, but does best in deeply worked, moist but well-drained soil that is rich in organic matter. Recommended pH range is 6.0 to 7.5. Keep plants watered during dry periods, otherwise the roots will become inferior.
- Prefers full sunlight, but will tolerate light shade.
  Horseradish grows most productively during late summer and early fall, as it is well adapted to cool weather.
- As horseradish does not grow from seed, buy plants from your local nursery. If you have access to existing plants, horseradish is easy to grow from root cuttings, which should be taken in the fall from the side roots, ideally when the plant is 2 years old. Cuttings should

be about 2.5 cm (1 inch) in diameter and about 8 cm (3 inches) long. Mark the upper end of the cutting (for example, cut upper end square, lower end diagonally) as the upper end should be planted uppermost, with the actual cutting planted out at an angle. Tie the cuttings in bundles, pack them in sand, and then store in a cool, moist location over the winter. In early spring, plant the cuttings with their upper ends about 8 cm (3 inches) below the surface of the soil.

- For the average home garden, 4 to 6 plants are plenty.
- Susceptible to root rot and the horseradish flea beetle.
- Although horseradish is a perennial, it is usually cultivated as an annual or biennial because if left indefinitely, the flavor diminishes and the plants become difficult to control. If you maintain your plants for more than a couple of years, you should divide the roots every 2 to 3 years to keep the plants vigorous.
- Overwinters outdoors up to zone 3.

> *Armoracia is thought to derive from Armorica,*
> *an ancient name for Britain, where horseradish grows wild.*

HARVESTING NOTES
- Harvest roots in late fall when they are tastiest, and keep in cool, moist sand for fresh use as needed. Alternatively, store the roots in perforated plastic vegetable bags in the refrigerator.
- To harvest roots from a plant grown as a perennial, scrape away the soil from the sides of the plant and cut off the small roots growing from the main root. Store as above.
- Harvest young spring leaves from overwintered plants as soon as possible. As the leaves turn dark green, they quickly become inedible.
- To produce a crop of blanched, forced leaves, place some roots with the crowns in moist soil in a warm, dark location. Harvest the resulting tender, sweet, white leaves when they are 10 to 15 cm (4 to 6 inches) long, usually in 2 to 3 weeks.

> *The German for horseradish is Meerrettich, meaning "sea radish," an allusion to its*
> *habit of growing near the sea. The English rendition of the German was*
> *"mareradish," which over time was transformed into "horseradish."*

CULINARY USES
- Horseradish roots need to be used fresh, as they lose their pungent, biting taste when cooked. To prepare the roots for culinary use, wash, clean, and scrape them. The roots can then be grated or sliced into thin strips. (As the roots give off a highly pungent, penetrating odor, be prepared for tears.) Once grated, use horseradish immediately or mix it in vinegar,

as the root darkens and loses its pungency and becomes unpleasantly bitter when exposed to air and heat.

- Combine grated horseradish root with white wine vinegar, some sugar and spices, and whipped cream to make horseradish sauce, the traditional accompaniment to roast beef. (Don't use cider vinegar as it will discolor the horseradish.) Keep the horseradish sauce in the refrigerator. Horseradish sauce is also delicious with ham and tongue, and vegetables such as broccoli.
- Add grated horseradish to tomato-based sauces to accompany fish, especially oily fish such as mackerel, and use it in shrimp dishes.
- Squeeze a few drops of juice from grated horseradish root to spice up coleslaw, applesauce, prepared mustards, cottage cheese, dips, appetizers, and relishes.
- Cook sliced horseradish roots and serve as a substitute for parsnips.
- Enliven salads by adding young spring leaves or blanched leaves produced by forcing.

> *Horseradish is at its pungent best in cool weather, so it's not surprising that some of the most potent horseradish comes from the region of Tuli Lakes, California, where there is frost every month of the year.*

MEDICINAL USES

- In traditional folk medicine, horseradish was used to treat a variety of ailments including asthma, coughs, colic, toothache, ulcers, venereal disease, cancer, worms, chilblains, neuralgia, and rheumatism. Horseradish root infused in wine was taken to stimulate the nervous system and to promote perspiration, while a poultice of grated roots served as an alternative to a mustard plaster.
- In modern medicine, extract of horseradish peroxidase is used for the diagnosis of the AIDS virus.
- Horseradish is rich in vitamin C, and high in vitamin K, calcium, fiber, iron, potassium, protein, and starch.

> *Two old standbys for removing freckles include the application of a mix of horseradish juice and white vinegar, and a rather odorous face wash of grated horseradish and very sour milk.*

CAUTIONS

- Applying horseradish directly to the skin may cause skin blisters in some people.
- Horseradish contains chemicals that can interfere with the thyroid gland's production of hormones, which can result in an enlarged thyroid gland. This isn't a risk for healthy individuals, but people with thyroid conditions should not eat horseradish.
- Consuming large amounts of horseradish may cause vomiting and diarrhea. Because horseradish irritates mucous membranes, young children and people with kidney, stomach, or intestinal disorders should consume it in limited amounts only.
- Do not feed horseradish leaves or roots to pets or livestock, as the results can be fatal.
- Although commercial horseradish oil is occasionally used for culinary and medicinal purposes, it is too potent to be kept in the home.

HYSSOP *Hyssopus officinalis*
Labiatae (Lamiaceae; mint family)
Also known as: Common hyssop, garden hyssop

Zone 2 Coldest Tolerated

DESCRIPTION

- Hyssop, a very attractive, cold-hardy, semi-woody, perennial sub-shrub, grows from 20 to 70 cm (8 inches to 28 inches) tall. It is native to Morocco, Algeria, southern Europe, Turkey, the Caucasus of Georgia, Iran to southern Siberia, and the western Himalayas. With its lovely bluish floral spires, hyssop can be grown for its beauty alone, whether as a part of your herb garden or as a becoming hedge.
- Nearly evergreen, smooth, slender leaves are pointed and opposite, with an aroma that is reminiscent of camphor and mint. The penetrating but light flavor is a cross between rosemary and savory, but it's not strongly camphoric like the former or bitter like the latter.
- Hyssop has many upright, downy, woody stems, and a strongly branching, multi-headed taproot.
- Produces whorls of small, deep bluish-violet flowers on tall spikes. Cultivars offer flowers in white, rose, pink, and red. Flavor and aroma are similar to the leaves. Hyssop blooms from midsummer to early fall.
- May also be grown outdoors in pots.
- Hyssop is very attractive to honeybees.
- Both leaves and flowers may be eaten.

CULTIVATION NOTES

- Hyssop grows well in dry, rocky, limestone soils, but will thrive in any light, well-drained soil. Although hyssop is not sensitive to soil conditions, and grows well in poor soils, older plants benefit from the addition of nitrogen-rich fertilizer early in the season. Recommended pH range is 5.0 to 7.5.
- Prefers a sunny location, but will grow in partial shade.
- Grows easily from seed, which should be planted outdoors a couple of weeks before your last spring frost date.
- Plant seeds no more than 1 cm (½ inch) deep. Seedlings usually emerge within 2 to 3 weeks, although some seeds can remain dormant for months.
- Can also be propagated from cuttings of young growth taken in late spring or early fall, or from root divisions made in early spring or late summer.
- Space plants 30 cm (12 inches) apart.

- To encourage new growth, cut the stems back to the ground in the fall or spring of each year.
- Discard or divide and re-establish your hyssop plants every 3 or 4 years, as the plants become woody and produce less foliage.
- Usually pest- and disease-free, but susceptible to root rot in soggy soil.
- Overwinters outdoors up to zone 2 (but should be mulched to overwinter in the coldest zone).

Pious ladies in various European countries used to press hyssop in their prayer books in the belief that the strong aroma would keep them awake during services.

HARVESTING NOTES
- Harvest leaves before the plant flowers, collecting them in the morning after the dew has evaporated.
- For fresh use, break off a portion of the stem, and remove the leaves.
- Pick fresh flowers for immediate use when they are almost fully open.
- To dry hyssop, harvest the tender upper stems and flowering shoots, and hang upside down in bunches to air dry. When dry, strip off leaves and flowers, crush, and store in an airtight container.

CULINARY USES
- Use hyssop flowers and leaves to season vegetable dishes, soups, casseroles, sauces, pickles, stuffing for meats and poultry, and to give salads, including fruit salad, a refreshing minty flavor. Use sparingly, as the taste can be quite strong.
- For a relaxing tea, steep 5 mL (1 teaspoon) of dried hyssop leaves and/or flowers in 250 mL (1 cup) of boiling water. Sweeten with honey to taste. For a lighter-flavored tea, mix hyssop with spearmint or lemon balm.
- Hyssop is used commercially in liqueurs such as Benedictine and Chartreuse.

CRAFT USES
- Add fresh or dried flowers to floral arrangements.
- Include fragrant dried leaves and flowers in potpourris and sachets.

According to Sicilian legend, hyssop should be used to ward off the evil eye and any evil magic.

MEDICINAL USES

- In traditional folk medicine, hyssop was used to treat asthma, bruises, ulcers, and rheumatism. It is not used today for any of these conditions.
- In modern medicine, an infusion of hyssop is considered reasonably helpful in treating the mild respiratory irritations that often accompany the common cold.
- Research studies indicate that hyssop extracts may be effective against *Herpes simplex* and HIV, but much more research is needed to establish whether this is a useful treatment.

CAUTIONS

- Hyssop has some capacity to stimulate menstruation and induce miscarriage, although only when consumed in large medicinal doses. As a precaution, if you are pregnant or suffer from a menstrual disorder, you should avoid consuming large quantities of this herb.
- As the plant tops and flowers are especially high in iodine, you should avoid them if you have iodine-related health problems, such as goiter.
- Bees like hyssop, so be careful there are none on the flowers you pick.

The generic name "hyssopus" comes from the Greek form of the Hebrew ezov, which botanical experts think may have been a collective term for several food plants grown in the Holy Land, in particular Syrian oregano. In the Bible, Psalm 51 alludes to hyssop's cleansing properties: "Purge me with hyssop and I shall be clean." In the Passover story, Moses commands the Israelites to take a bunch of hyssop and dip it in the blood of a lamb to sprinkle on their doorposts and lintels, and then remain in their homes until morning. Whether the hyssop in question was actually Hyssopus officinalis is a moot point.

HYSSOP, ANISE *Agastache foeniculum*
Labiatae (Lamiaceae; mint family)

Also known as: Blue giant hyssop, elk mint, fragrant giant hyssop, lavender giant hyssop, licorice mint

Zone **4**

Coldest Tolerated

DESCRIPTION

- Anise hyssop, a stiffly erect perennial that grows from 0.6 to 1.5 m (2 to 5 feet) tall, is native to North America. Because it is as lovely as it is aromatic, this herb is also often grown in flower gardens, where it makes a very attractive background plant.
- Pointed, bright green leaves have serrated edges, and are covered with soft, white, felt-like hairs underneath. In the spring, new foliage often has a pretty purplish cast. Aroma and flavor are an intriguing mix of anise and mint.
- Anise hyssop has branched, mostly hairless stems. The spreading rootstock bears fibrous roots.
- Produces longish flower spikes made up of many beautiful little lilac-blue blossoms from July to September. A white flowered cultivar is also available Flowers have a lighter flavor than the leaves.
- Anise hyssop is very attractive to honey-bees, and is widely cultivated as a honey plant. It is also a source of nectar for butterflies, while its seeds attract wild birds, especially finches.
- Both flowers and leaves may be eaten.

CULTIVATION NOTES

- Anise hyssop grows best in well-drained, fertile soils containing compost or well-rotted manure. In its natural habitat, it thrives in soils that retain moisture, but are not excessively wet.
- Prefers full sunlight, but will tolerate light shade. Plants must be kept moist during dry weather, otherwise they will stop flowering in late summer.
- Does best in cool weather.
- Sow seeds indoors in the early spring. Seeds are quite small and can successfully germinate under a light covering of soil, so they should be planted to a

depth of no more than 6 mm (¼ inch). Seeds usually germinate in 4 to 10 days. Plant seedlings outdoors when all danger of frost is past.

- Space plants 30 cm (12 inches) apart.
- Seeds can also be planted outside in late fall and allowed to lie dormant through the winter, to germinate in the early spring.
- Alternatively, you can establish new plantings in the spring from divisions of established plants. Root cuttings from soft or semi-ripe stems.
- Anise hyssop grows very slowly initially, and often takes 2 years from seed to bloom.
- Pinch back plants in early summer to encourage branching.
- Generally pest- and disease-free.
- Overwinters outdoors up to zone 4.

> *The genus name Agastache comes from the Greek agan and stachys, meaning "many ears of wheat," an allusion to the profusion of tiny blossoms that make up the flower spikes.*

HARVESTING NOTES

- Harvest leaves for fresh or dried use throughout the growing season. Collect leaves on sunny, dry days, preferably in the morning. Cut off leaves for fresh use as needed, starting at the bottom of the plant.
- To dry anise hyssop, cut whole stems about 10 cm (4 inches) from the base of the plant. Hang stems upside down in a shady location to air-dry. Strip dried leaves and store in an airtight container.
- Pick fresh leaves and flowers for tea throughout the growing season.
- If drying for tea, cut the stems 15 cm (6 inches) from the base of the plant. Include flowers with the stems. Hang upside down to air-dry. Store dried material in an airtight container.

CULINARY USES

- Add fresh leaves and flowers to salads and fruit salads, and use as a garnish.
- Use fresh or dried leaves to complement lamb, chicken, salmon, and to enliven vegetables such as peas. Substitute anise hyssop leaves in recipes calling for anise or mint.
- Use flowers in baking, especially in tea breads.

Cultivar Alba

- Add fresh young leaves to cool summer drinks.
- To make a refreshing cup of anise hyssop tea, add 5 mL (1 teaspoon) of dried leaves and flowers or 15 mL (3 teaspoons) of fresh leaves and flowers to 250 mL (1 cup) of boiling water. Cover and steep for 10 minutes. Strain and sweeten with honey to taste.
- Light-colored anise hyssop honey is quite delicious.
- Anise hyssop essential oil is used commercially to flavor root beer and various liqueurs.

CRAFT USES
- Include lovely anise hyssop blooms in fresh or dried floral arrangements.
- Add fragrant dried flowers to potpourris and sachets.

MEDICINAL USES
- In traditional herbal medicine, anise hyssop tea was used to aid digestion. Anise hyssop is not used in modern medicine.

CAUTIONS
- Bees love anise hyssop, so be careful there are none on the flowers you pick to bring indoors.

For centuries, native North Americans turned to anise hyssop for medicinal purposes. The Cheyenne used an infusion of the leaves for colds, coughs, and chest pain, and rubbed powdered leaves on the body to help reduce fevers, while the Chippewa treated burns with a poultice made from the leaves or stalks. Anise hyssop flowers were often included in Cree medicine bundles.

JUNIPER *Juniperus communis*
Cupressaceae (cypress family)
Also known as: Common juniper, melmot berry, mountain berry

DESCRIPTION

- Juniper, a very variable, hardy species that makes an ideal garden ornamental or foundation plant, is native to North America and Eurasia. Depending on habitat, this highly aromatic evergreen can be found as an erect shrub, a low-spreading shrub that makes attractive ground cover, or as a pyramid- or column-shaped small tree that grows up to 10 m (33 feet) tall.
- Blue-green, small, needle-like leaves are 1 cm (½ inch) long. Arranged in three's, the leaves have a pine-like smell.
- Small cones, some male, others female, develop in early summer at the base of a few of the leaves. Male cones are yellow, while female cones are hard, pungent, and bluish-green with a whitish, waxy coating. The female cones ripen into fleshy berries, gradually turning from green to blue-black. Berries take 2 (sometimes 3) years to ripen. A ripe berry contains up to 6 seeds.
- As juniper plants usually produce either male or female cones, you will need a male and a female plant in order to have berries.
- Juniper berries, which are edible, have a sweet, pungent, slightly burning taste, with a distinctive bittersweet aroma that is reminiscent of gin, pine, and turpentine.
- May also be grown outdoors in pots and containers.

CULTIVATION NOTES

- Junipers grow naturally on dry, rocky soil. For a taller shrub, plant in rich, well-drained soil. Tolerated pH range is 4.5 to 7.5.
- Does best in an open, sunny location.
- While it is possible to grow juniper from seed sown in the fall, the seeds take a long time to germinate. It's easier to propagate juniper from cuttings, which should be planted in spring or fall.
- Trim plants as needed to prevent them from becoming scraggly. Be careful not to cut into the old wood.
- Susceptible to insect pests such as bagworms, aphids, and scale, and to fungus diseases such as rust and Phomopsis blight.
- Overwinters outdoors up to zone 2.

According to the Old Testament, the prophet Elijah took refuge under a juniper tree to escape persecution by King Ahab.

HARVESTING NOTES

- Pick juniper berries when they are completely ripe, usually towards the end of summer.
- Spread the berries out thinly on a tray and dry in the sun, or in an airy, shady location. When the berries are dry and shriveled, store them in an airtight container.
- For maximum flavor, use dried berries within a year of harvesting.

During epidemics of plague and smallpox, people used to burn juniper in the streets and in their homes in the hope that it would purify the air and ward off infection.

CULINARY USES

- Crushed juniper berries, either fresh or dried, are excellent in marinades and conserves to serve with cold meats. Their aromatic, resinous flavor adds gusto to wild game, beef, pork, goose, pickled fish, casseroles, stuffing, pâté, gravies, and hearty vegetable dishes such as sauerkraut.
- Grind dried berries in a pepper mill and use as an alternative to pepper. Add to recipes that you customarily season with marjoram, rosemary, garlic, or other aromatic herbs, but use sparingly, as the flavor is strong.
- Burn juniper wood to flavor and cure smoked meat and fish.
- Juniper berries are used commercially to flavor gin and various liqueurs.

"Juniper" comes from the Celtic word jenupus, meaning "bitter."

CRAFT USES

- Use the berries and roots to make brown and purple dyes.

MEDICINAL USES

- Juniper was used in traditional herbal medicine to treat a number of conditions ranging from arthritis, colic, and cancer to venereal diseases, worms, and warts. It is not considered to be useful medically today.

It takes 1 kg (2.2 pounds) of juniper berries to flavor 400 L (about 106 American gallons) of gin.

CAUTIONS

- Some juniper species produce berries that are unsuitable for culinary use. Widely planted ornamental evergreen yew trees and shrubs (of the genus *Taxus*), which can be mistaken for juniper, produce berries with seeds that can be deadly poisonous. While junipers are extremely common, if you aren't certain of the plant's identity, don't eat the berries.
- Don't use juniper oil to flavor food, as the oil of some juniper species is extremely poisonous.
- As potential side effects from self-medicating with juniper are dangerous, you should not use this herb as medicine.
- Juniper acts as a diuretic (stimulates urination) and has often been used as a herbal remedy for premenstrual syndrome; however, this use is not recommended as it may cause kidney and bladder irritation.
- Because of its diuretic effects, you should not eat juniper if you suffer from kidney disease.
- If you are diabetic, you should be aware that eating juniper berries can raise your glucose level.
- If you are pregnant, you should not eat juniper, as it may cause uterine contractions, and in rare cases, can result in abortion.
- Some people may experience contact dermatitis after handling juniper.
- Wear gloves when harvesting juniper because the leaves are quite prickly.

During their flight into Egypt, the Virgin Mary and the infant Jesus are said to have hidden from Herod's army behind a juniper tree.

In Medieval Europe, it was customary to plant a juniper tree by the front door to keep witches out — unless they correctly counted the number of its needles.

LAVENDER, ENGLISH *Lavandula angustifolia*
Labiatae (Lamiaceae; mint family)

Also known as: Common lavender, garden lavender, old English lavender, sweet lavender, true lavender

Zone 5

Coldest Tolerated

DESCRIPTION

- English lavender, a sweet-smelling, hardy, ornamental perennial that grows from 30 to 90 cm (1 to 3 feet) tall, was brought to North America by the Pilgrims. This pretty herb, which is found from the Atlantic Islands and Mediterranean region to northern tropical Africa, western Asia, Arabia, and India, makes a fragrant border for garden pathways and deserves a place in sunny rock gardens.
- Narrow, bluish-green, opposite, stalkless leaves are often whitish when young, giving the plant its characteristic silvery-gray hue. The smooth-edged leaves, which can be up to 5 cm (2 inches) long, have a bitter, aromatic flavor and aroma.
- Lavender has short, upright, many-branched stems that grow from a woody base. The roots, which can grow as deep as 4 m (13 feet), form a main woody system that is densely branched at the bottom.
- Produces graceful spikes of tiny mauve or gray-blue flowers that grow in whorls of 6 to 8 blooms. (Cultivars offer purple, pink, or white flowers.) Spikes may be up to 30 cm (1 foot) long. Intensely fragrant and very pleasantly perfumed, lavender blooms from midsummer to early fall.
- May also be grown outdoors in pots and containers.
- Lavender is extremely attractive to bees and butterflies.
- Both flowers and leaves may be eaten.

CULTIVATION NOTES

- Lavender tolerates various types of soils, but does best in dry, sandy, well-drained alkaline soil. If planting in acidic soil, neutralize it first with ground limestone. Tolerated pH range is 6.4 to 8.2.
- Requires full sun. Do not plant lavender in a shady, damp location as it will not develop or flower well.
- Start seeds indoors about 10 to 12 weeks before your last spring frost date. To increase the speed of germination, chill the seeds in the refrigerator for several weeks before planting.

(Refrigerated seeds should be kept moist.) Plant seeds no deeper than 6 mm (¼ inch). Seeds take from 14 to 28 days to germinate. Plant seedlings outside after all danger of frost is past.

- Plants grown from seeds are often variable and may not reproduce the distinctive characteristics of the cultivar.
- Because seeds of many cultivars take up to 6 weeks to germinate, and the seedlings grow very slowly, it's easier to propagate lavender from stem cuttings, which should be taken in spring or fall.
- Space plants 30 to 90 cm (1 to 3 feet) apart.
- Add liquid fertilizer regularly to potted plants to encourage flowering.
- Although English lavender can live 20 to 30 years, it becomes untidy after a few years, so trim plants back in spring and again in early fall.
- For more compact plants, nip off the flower spikes before they bloom during the first year.
- Susceptible to infestations of spittle bugs and caterpillars, and to fungus diseases such as leaf spot. Plants in overly moist soil are also prone to root rot. Improve drainage and minimize the likelihood of disease by planting in raised beds. Prune near the stem to improve air circulation around the base of the plant.
- Overwinters outdoors up to zone 5. Plants left outdoors should be covered with mulch, straw, or evergreen boughs to protect them from the cold.

The ancient Egyptians made mummification casts that would last indefinitely by soaking linen in oil of lavender containing asphalt, wrapping the dead in this linen, and then drying the swathed corpses in the sun until the casts hardened.

HARVESTING NOTES
- Harvest leaves at any time for fresh use in the kitchen.
- Pick flowers before the last blooms on each stalk are fully open. It's best to harvest the stalks on a dry day, before the heat of the sun evaporates much of the essential oils. Tie the stalks in bundles and hang them in a warm, shady, airy place to dry. (The drying process may take several weeks.) When the stalks are crisp, strip the flowers from the stems and store in airtight containers. Stalks may also be dried flat on cookie sheets.
- For potpourri use, pick the flowers for drying just as the buds start to open.

Lavandula comes from the Latin lavo, meaning "I wash," from the frequent use the ancient Romans made of lavender water perfume, which was made from oil of lavender.

CULINARY USES

- Use dried lavender – leaves, buds, and flowers – to season meat and vegetable dishes.
- Add flowering tips and freshly chopped leaves to dressings, salads, wine, and vinegar.
- Flavor desserts such as ice cream, jellies, puddings, and fruit, especially berries, with lavender blossoms. English lavender's sweet lemon-floral taste can be quite intense, so use sparingly.
- To make refreshing, aromatic lavender tea, steep 5 mL (1 teaspoon) of dried flowers or 15 mL (3 teaspoons) of fresh flowers in 250 mL (1 cup) of boiling water.
- Lavender honey is deservedly considered a gourmet's delight.
- *Herbes de Provence*, the classic dried herb blend, contains lavender blossoms as well as thyme, savory, basil, and fennel.
- Lavender oil extract is used commercially to flavor candy, baked goods, chewing gum, gelatins, puddings, and various beverages.

Fragrant lavender oil extract is widely used in the cosmetic industry in perfumes, lotions, conditioners for oily hair, shaving creams, and soaps. Most commercially produced lavender oil comes from hybrids of English lavender and spike lavender (L. latifolia).

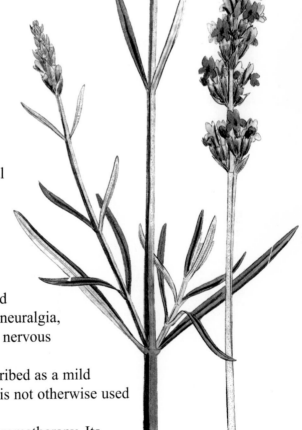

CRAFT USES

- Include graceful lavender spikes in fresh floral arrangements.
- Dried lavender spikes remain aromatic for a number of years, making them ideal for long-lasting sachets and potpourris.

MEDICINAL USES

- In traditional folk medicine, lavender was used for treating many conditions, including colic, neuralgia, nausea, flatulence, acne, rheumatism, sprains, nervous palpitations, and worms.
- Although lavender drugs are sometimes prescribed as a mild sedative in modern herbal medicine, the herb is not otherwise used medicinally.
- Lavender is the most important herb used in aromatherapy. Its fragrance is said to calm nerves and relax tension.

Hanging bunches of lavender throughout the home helps deter flies and mosquitoes, while putting dried lavender in clothing and linen closets helps repel moths, as well as imparting a wonderful scent.

CAUTIONS

- Some people can experience dermatitis from lavender oil.
- Lavender oil is widely available for aromatherapy, and a couple of drops are sometimes used to make tea. However, lavender oil should never be taken in large doses, as it is a narcotic poison that can cause convulsions and death. We recommend using the herb only (not the concentrated oil) for consumption.
- Make sure there are no bees on the lavender that you pick for household use.

From the 12th century on, lavender was widely employed to mask noxious household odors and to reduce the risk of disease.

CULTIVARS AND RELATIVES

Lavender was the International Herb Association's 1999 Herb of the Year. The English varieties are the most popular.

- 'Lady' (*L. angustifolia* 'Lady'). Flowers in the first year, even when grown from seed. Beautiful purplish-blue flowers. Grows 20 to 25 cm (8 to 10 inches) tall. Reliably hardy.
- 'Munstead' (*L. angustifolia* 'Munstead'). Lovely true lavender-blue flowers grow on short stems. Ideal for hedges as it grows no taller than about 45 cm (18 inches). Reliably hardy, but grows slower than 'Lady.'
- 'Hidcote' (*L. angustifolia* 'Hidcote'). Dwarf, compact, silvery-gray plant produces abundant deep purple flowers. Excellent for borders. Grows to 30 cm (12 inches) tall. Reliably hardy.

LOVAGE *Levisticum officinale*

Umbelliferae (Apiaceae; carrot family)

Also known as: Cornish lovage, Italian lovage, love parsley, sea parsley, old English lovage

Zone
4
Coldest Tolerated

DESCRIPTION

- Lovage is a dramatic, robust perennial that grows as tall as 2 m (6 feet), and eventually expands to a clump that's just as wide. Lovage, whose early arrival in the spring signals the end of winter, is native to the eastern Mediterranean and Afghanistan.
- When grown from seed, a rosette is formed in the first year. In subsequent years, a flowering stem develops.
- Glossy, dark green, celery-like, compound leaves have a strong scent and flavor of both celery and parsley, with a spicy tang.
- Lovage has hollow, ribbed stems that divide into branches near the top of the plant, and are often purplish at the base. The long, fleshy, brown root has a slightly nutty flavor.
- Produces umbrella-like clusters of tiny, greenish-yellow flowers in midsummer, followed by brown, caraway-like seeds.
- All parts of the plant may be eaten.

CULTIVATION NOTES

- Lovage is tolerant of most soils except heavy clay; however, it does best in deep, fertile soil that is well drained and also retains moisture. Add well-rotted manure once a year. Tolerated pH range is 5.0 to 7.6.
- Prefers full sunlight, but can grow in shade. Requires watering during dry periods.
- Grows easily from fresh seeds sown in late summer or fall. Seeds must be fresh in order to germinate, so plant them as soon as you acquire them.

- Plant seeds 6 mm (¼ inch) deep. Seedlings usually emerge in 10 to 28 days.
- Requires a full summer from seed to develop into a reasonably sized plant.
- Expands in size each subsequent year. As lovage is the biggest of the kitchen herbs, grow it on the north side of your garden, so that it won't shade smaller plants.
- If seeds are unavailable, plant nursery stock just before your last spring frost date. (A couple of plants are plenty for most gardens.) If there are plants already growing in your neighborhood, you can take a division from the outside of a mature plant, making sure to take a piece of root with an eye or bud.
- Space plants 60 cm (2 feet) apart.
- Self-sows readily, so cut off the fruiting stalk before the seeds mature and fall to the ground. If you don't, you'll be faced with a thick growth of new seedlings in the next growing season.
- Although lovage can live up to 8 years, you should divide and replant the fleshy rootstocks every 3 or 4 years to keep the plant vigorous. This is best done in early spring or late fall, when the plant is dormant.
- Susceptible to aphids, chewing insects, and fungal diseases. Sometimes leaf miners will leave whitish tunneling marks in some of the leaves. If this occurs, simply pick off and destroy the affected leaves.
- Overwinters outdoors up to zone 4, but survives best under mulch or snow cover.

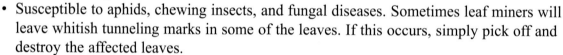

Lovage's generic name Levisticum is derived from an early Greek word for the Italian town of Liguria, where the plant once grew abundantly.

HARVESTING NOTES
- Pick leaves for fresh use at any time. Ideally, harvest the leaves in the morning when the dew has evaporated.
- To dry lovage, harvest stems with leaves before the plant begins to flower. Hang stems in a warm, dry, airy, shady location. When dry, strip leaves and store in an airtight container.
- To freeze lovage, blanch the leaves and then freeze in plastic freezer bags.
- To harvest seeds, cut the fruiting stalks in the late summer as they are turning brown. Enclose the seed heads in paper bags, or hang the stalks upside down over a cloth to catch the ripe seeds. Store dried seeds in an airtight container.

Lovage flowers are natural pest controllers, as they are attractive to tiny parasitic wasps whose young prey on garden pests such as cutworms and tent caterpillars.

The common names "lovage" and "love parsley" are derived from the herb's use in love potions. In a more romantic era, wearing a sachet of lovage and orris root was said to ensure the return of affection from one's secret love.

CULINARY USES

- Add lovage to soups, especially those containing potatoes, peas, beans, and lentils, and use to season stews, chili, chicken pot pie, stir-fried vegetables, and your favorite seafood recipes. Lovage makes a tasty addition to bland vegetables such as summer squash.
- Rub a salad bowl with lovage to impart a fresh celery taste to a crisp salad.
- Always chop lovage leaves finely, as they are inclined to be a little coarse.
- Lovage stalks are rather fibrous. When using them in cooking, be sure to remove before serving.
- Try blanching lovage leaf stalks and then eat them like celery.
- Blanched stalks may be candied and used to decorate cakes and desserts.
- Add whole or ground lovage seeds to candy, cakes, meats, breads, and savory crackers or biscuits. Seeds can also be pickled like capers.
- Grate fresh roots into salad or serve as a cooked vegetable, but peel first as the outer skin is bitter.
- Steep 5 mL (1 teaspoon) grated lovage root, fresh or dried, in 250 mL (1 cup) of boiling water for a hearty, energizing tea.

An old remedy for lancing boils called for the application of crushed lovage leaves that had been fried in hog fat.

MEDICINAL USES

- In traditional folk medicine, lovage was used to reduce flatulence and promote digestion. It is occasionally employed in current European herbal medicine to treat kidney ailments, but it is rarely used in modern medicine.
- Lovage increases urine production and is a basic ingredient of diuretic tea mixtures, especially in Europe.
- Lovage is rich in vitamin C.

The ancient Greeks chewed lovage seeds to aid digestion and relieve flatulence. In the Middle Ages, lovage was grown in monastery gardens both as a culinary herb and for its medicinal properties.

CAUTIONS

- Lovage may cause some people to experience photodermatitis, a skin rash that appears after consuming the herb and subsequently being exposed to sunlight.
- Because lovage increases urine flow, it is inadvisable for individuals with kidney problems.
- Lovage may stimulate menstruation and induce miscarriage if consumed in very large quantities, as is sometimes done for medicinal purposes. If you are pregnant or suffering from menstrual disorders, you should avoid large quantities of lovage.

MARIGOLD, POT *Calendula officinalis*

Compositae (Asteraceae; sunflower family)

Also known as: Bull flower, butterwort, care, cowbloom, common
marigold, death-flower, drunkard, golden flower of Mary, gouls, holygold,
poet's marigold, publican and sinner, Scotch marigold, shining herb,
summer's bride, water dragon

Annual

DESCRIPTION

- Pot marigold, known since antiquity as
  the saffron of the poor, is a colorful,
  bushy annual that grows from 30 to 60 cm
  (1 to 2 feet) tall. Native from the Canary Islands
  through south and central Europe and North
  Africa to Iran, pot marigold should not be
  confused with the many varieties of garden
  marigolds (*Tagetes*), such as Mexican, African,
  and French marigolds, which are so popular as
  bedding plants and as natural garden insect
  repellants. (Several kinds of *Tagetes* grown mostly in hot
  climates produce tasty flowers and sometimes also leaves.)
- Fleshy, pale green, narrow, oval leaves are covered in very
  soft hairs, and taste salty and somewhat bitter.
- Pot marigold has a many-branched, erect stem,
  and may be woody at the base. The spindle-
  shaped taproot is about 20 cm (8 inches)
  long.
- Produces abundant daisy-like blooms, varying
  through shades of yellow, orange, and orange-red, throughout
  the summer. Pot marigold belongs to the sunflower family, so
  its blooms are tiny and clustered into flower heads. These flower
  heads are commonly, though inaccurately, referred to as flowers.
  Each of the outermost flowers in the flower heads has a prominent
  strap-shaped petal, while the petals of the central flowers in the
  head are inconspicuous, except in cultivars whose flowers have been doubled by selection.
  The prominent peripheral petals are best for culinary use. Typical pot marigold has single
  flowers, which are preferred over the double forms for culinary purposes, although the latter
  do produce more of the desired prominent petals. The petals have a delicate, aromatic salty
  bitterness, with sweetish undertones.
- May be grown in containers or pots, both outdoors and indoors.
- Both flowers and young leaves may be eaten.

112

The generic name Calendula comes from the Latin calendae, the "calends" or first day of the month in the ancient Roman calendar. Pot marigold is said to have been in bloom on the calends of every month.

CULTIVATION NOTES
- Pot marigold grows best in light, sandy, moderately rich, fairly moist but well-drained soil. Tolerated pH range is 4.5 to 8.3.
- Prefers full sun, but will grow in light shade.
- Grows easily from seed, which should be planted in the garden in spring, when all danger of frost is past. Plant seeds 6 mm (¼ inch) deep. Seedlings usually emerge in 8 to 12 days.
- Do not transplant the seedlings, as this often causes their large succulent leaves to wilt.
- Thin seedlings to about 40 to 50 cm (16 to 20 inches) between plants.
- As the plants grow, remove side branches to encourage taller growth and larger blooms. Remove dead flower heads to keep plants flowering throughout the summer.
- If left undisturbed, pot marigold will self-sow.
- Usually pest- and disease-free.
- Pot outdoor plants for indoor use by midsummer. Bring plants indoors several days before your estimated first fall frost date. Indoor plants require at least 5 hours of direct sunlight or 12 hours of strong artificial light each day. Avoid overwatering, which can cause root rot. Keep the soil barely moist.

The French for marigold, gauche-fer, which means "left-hand iron," came about because the brilliant yellow flower resembled the polished shields that warriors once wore on their left arm.

HARVESTING NOTES
- Pick young leaves only for fresh use.
- Collect pot marigold petals for fresh or dried use as the flowers are opening. For fresh use, pluck the petals from the flowers, cut off the white or pale green "heels," which are rather bitter, wash the petals gently, and drain well. Alternatively, wash the picked flowers, pluck the individual petals, and pat dry with paper towels. Store petals in plastic bags in the refrigerator for use as needed.
- To dry pot marigold, spread out the harvested flowers thinly on screens in a dark, warm, well-ventilated location. (The petals lose color and flavor if ventilation during drying is poor.) Turn the flowers frequently until they are crisp. When the petals are dry, separate them from the flowers, and store in an airtight container. (As pot marigold petals absorb water vapor, they must be quite dry before being stored.) The dried petals can also be crushed and used as a powder.

In India, Buddhists believed that pot marigold was sacred to the goddess Mahadevi, who carried a trident emblem adorned with the flowers. Mahadevi's followers would crown themselves with marigolds at her festival.

Pot marigold flowers tend to open at sunrise and close in the afternoon, a fact noted by Shakespeare in The Winter's Tale: "The marigold that goes to bed wi' th' sun, And with him rises weeping." In German folklore, if pot marigold flowers have not opened by 7:00 a.m., it is a sure sign that rain is on the way.

CULINARY USES

- Add fresh young leaves to your favorite salads, and sprinkle tossed salads with chopped fresh flower petals.
- Use the petals, fresh, dried, or powdered, to impart color and a subtle bittersweet flavor to seafood, chowders, soups, stews, rice, roast meats, vegetable dishes, and chicken.
- To make a flavoring liquid from the petals, chop and bruise the petals, then soak them in milk or water. Strain the golden liquid and use as required.
- Substitute pot marigold in recipes calling for saffron. The color is similarly vibrant, but the flavor is different, and while saffron is costly, pot marigold is not.
- Pot marigold flowers are used commercially to color poultry products, butter and cheese, and to flavor ice cream, soft drinks, baked goods, and candy.

CRAFT USES

- Cut pretty pot marigold throughout the summer for inclusion in fresh floral bouquets and arrangements.
- Use the fragrant flower heads and petals in potpourris.

MEDICINAL USES

- In traditional folk medicine, pot marigold was used to treat warts, menstrual conditions, fevers, smallpox, measles, sprains, cancer, varicose veins, boils, and inflamed eyes. Rubbing the fresh flowers on bee and wasp stings was said to help relieve the pain and swelling.
- In Europe, pot marigold preparations are widely used for treating skin inflammations, wounds that are slow to heal, mild burns, and sunburn.
- Pot marigold is used commercially in personal care products such as soap, skin lotion, cosmetics, perfume, and shampoo.

CAUTIONS

- Pot marigold is one of the safest of culinary herbs, but if you are allergic to the pollen of species of the daisy family, such as ragweed, you may experience an allergic reaction to pot marigold, although it's not very likely.
- Pot marigold is often used in homemade skin preparations as it is considered very safe and is mildly therapeutic. Some individuals may develop an allergic reaction from frequent skin contact with this herb, but again this is not very common.
- Pot marigold is traditionally thought to influence the menstrual cycle. As a result, some authorities recommend that pregnant women and nursing mothers avoid consuming pot marigold, although there is no evidence of harm to date.

MARJORAM, SWEET *Origanum majorana*

Labiatae (Lamiaceae; mint family)

Also known as: Amaracus, annual marjoram, knotted marjoram

Annual

DESCRIPTION

- Sweet marjoram, oregano's more subtly flavored cousin, is a tender perennial that is grown as an annual in northern gardens. Believed to be native to North Africa, the Middle East, and part of India, sweet marjoram grows from 25 to 60 cm (10 to 24 inches) tall. A pretty herb with a rather bushy, sprawling habit, sweet marjoram makes an attractive hanging plant and is ideal for borders and rock gardens.
- Abundant, small, round, fuzzy-haired, opposite leaves are grayish-green and have a sweet, spicy fragrance and flavor.
- Sweet marjoram has a purplish, square stem and many wiry branches, and a thin main root with side branches.
- Produces clusters of dainty white or pink flowers that appear on spikes at the ends of the branches in late summer to early fall. Before they open, the flower buds resemble knots, hence the herb's common name "knotted marjoram."
- May be grown in pots and containers, both outside and indoors.
- Leaves, flowers, and tender stems may all be eaten.

CULTIVATION NOTES

- Sweet marjoram grows best in rich, light, well-drained soil. Tolerated pH range is 4.9 to 8.7.
- Prefers full sunlight, but will tolerate slight shade.
- Start seeds indoors about 6 to 8 weeks before your last spring frost date. Plant seeds to a depth of 6 mm (¼ inch) or less. Keep the soil evenly moist during germination. Seeds are slow to germinate, but seedlings will usually appear in 8 to 15 days. Move the tiny seedlings into a sunny position, and transplant them to the garden after all danger of frost is passed.
- Space plants 15 to 20 cm (6 to 8 inches) apart.
- Outdoor plants require regular watering during the vegetative growth phase.

- Pinch back the tops of the plants to encourage branching and promote bushy growth.
- Susceptible to root rot, fungal diseases, spider mites, aphids, and leaf miners, and to damping-off in early spring.
- Sweet marjoram overwinters well indoors. Pot plants in fall in dry, free-draining, sandy soil. Water well and then allow the soil to dry—but not dry out—between waterings. Do not overwater. Place plants in a sunny location, as sweet marjoram requires at least 5 hours of direct sunlight daily. Pinch off flower buds to stimulate leaf growth.
- Put indoor plants back out in the garden after the last spring frost.

The ancient Greeks used sweet marjoram as an antidote for snakebite. Even if the patient died, the Greeks remained firm in their belief in the value of sweet marjoram, and planted it on the grave of the deceased to help the unlucky individual sleep peacefully.

HARVESTING NOTES

- Pick leaves for fresh use at any time after the plant is 15 to 20 cm (6 to 8 inches) tall.
- Harvest leaves and stems for drying just after the flower buds form or just before flowering, when the flavor is at its peak. Cut the stems close to the ground and tie in bunches. Hang bunches in a warm, dry, shady location to dry. Strip dried leaves from the stems and store in airtight containers out of the light. Unlike many herbs, sweet marjoram's flavor becomes more intense when dried.
- Freeze leaves in butter or oil.

CULINARY USES

- Sweet marjoram improves the flavor of most dishes and is a popular kitchen standby when the chef is not sure which herb to use. It is deceptively potent, however, so use it sparingly.
- Add young shoots and leaves to salads and vegetable recipes calling for carrots, mushrooms, cauliflower, peas, spinach, summer squash, and cabbage. Use sweet marjoram in pizza and tomato sauces, beef and pork dishes, and to season soups, stews, sausages, meat pies, stuffing, omelets, poultry, and seafood.
- Add sweet marjoram to hot dishes only in the last 10 minutes of cooking.
- The leaves, flowers, and tender stems are used commercially to flavor syrups, dressings, liqueurs, sauces, and vinegar, while the seeds are used in candy, beverages, condiments, and processed meats.

CRAFT USES

- Include sweet marjoram in potpourris and in sachets for your linen and clothing cupboards.

Origanum comes from the Greek oras, *meaning "mountain," and* ganos, *meaning "joy." The sight and smell of pretty, fragrant marjoram growing wild on the hillsides caused this herb to be so appropriately named "joy of the mountain."*

MEDICINAL USES

- In traditional folk medicine, sweet marjoram was used as a remedy for asthma, indigestion, headache, rheumatism, toothache, earache, flatulence, epilepsy, and to help relieve the pain of childbirth. The oil was used as a liniment for sprains and bruises and to promote perspiration in those suffering from the measles.
- Sweet marjoram is rarely used in modern medicine; however, in Europe, it is occasionally used to treat rhinitis and colds in infants.

CAUTIONS

- In Europe, marjoram salve is sometimes available to treat bruises. It should never be applied to infants or small children, and is of doubtful value because it contains a carcinogenic compound (hydroxyquinone) which can de-pigment the skin.

According to Greek legend, Aphrodite, the goddess of love, first cultivated sweet marjoram and its lovely scent came from her touch. The Roman version of this legend is that Venus, the goddess of love and beauty, left the perfume of marjoram to remind mortals of her loveliness. Since antiquity, sweet marjoram has been a symbol of happiness, and both the Greeks and Romans followed the custom of crowning newly weds with the fragrant herb.

MINTS

Mentha species
Labiatae (Lamiaceae; mint family)

PEPPERMINT & SPEARMINT

OTHER SPECIES

Zone
3
Coldest
Tolerated

Zone
5
Coldest
Tolerated

DESCRIPTION

- Many species with a minty taste or fragrance have "mint" in their names, but the true mints are species of the genus *Mentha*. Important flavoring and medicinal herbs since antiquity, mints are mostly highly aromatic, easy-to-cultivate, hardy perennials. Mints, which originated in Europe and Asia, generally grow from 30 to 90 cm (12 to 36 inches) tall, although some are ground hugging.
- Leaves in most varieties are opposite, plentiful, toothed, and pointed. Depending on type, mint leaves come in many hues of green, some mottled spectacularly with gold. Fragrance and flavor are just as varied, ranging from refreshing, tangy peppermint to sweetish, fruity apple.
- Mints have square stems, and most species have creeping underground rhizomes (underground stems), which bear slim roots at intervals.
- Most types produce terminal spikes of dainty, purple, pink, or white flowers. Plants usually bloom in mid- to late summer.
- Can be grown in pots or containers, both outside and indoors, although indoor plants tend to become scraggy. Apple mint, however, grows into an attractive, compact, houseplant.

CULTIVATION NOTES

- Mints grow best in moist, deep, loosely textured sandy soil that is rich in humus. Recommended pH range for peppermint is 6.0 to 7.5; for spearmint, the pH range is 5.5 to 7.0.
- Many mints, including peppermint and spearmint, thrive in full sun, but also do very well in partial shade. Some mints, like water mint, tolerate considerable shade. Corsican mint must have shade. In northern areas, mints won't develop their best flavor and fragrance if not grown in full sun. Keep well watered.

Peppermint

- May be grown from seed, but this is not advisable, as most mints do not come true from seed.
- Propagate mints from cuttings taken from established plants before they bloom, or by dividing existing plants, optimally in the early spring, or buy from nurseries or garden catalogs.
- Space plants 45 cm (18 inches) apart.
- Once established, mints spread very quickly by underground runners or stolons. To prevent mints from taking over your herb garden, plan on digging up unwanted runners each spring, or curb the runners by sinking drainage tiles or plastic dividers in the soil around the plants, to a minimum depth of about 30 cm (12 inches). Or plant mints in large containers or pots with drainage holes, sunk in the ground.
- Pinch off the flowers to promote bushy growth.
- Renew mints every 3 years by dividing and replanting the roots in the spring or fall. Peppermint, in particular, does not grow well in the same location for more than a few years, and should be moved to a new spot.
- Susceptible to infestations of aphids, cutworms, spider mites, and mint flea beetles, as well as verticillium wilt disease and rust, if the soil is too rich. Diseased plants should be dug up and burned promptly. Replant next season in a different location.
- Peppermint and spearmint overwinter outdoors reliably up to zone 4, and can also be grown in zone 3 with protection. Most other species can be grown up to zone 5, but some require winter mulch or a protected location. Where winters are usually harsh, cover the plants with straw (but not soil) to prevent damage to the runners.
- Establish indoor plants in commercial potting soil in the spring or early fall. Containers or pots need to be large enough to give the creeping roots sufficient room to develop.
- Indoor plants need at least 5 hours of strong sunlight daily. Keep the soil most but not soggy. Apply a liquid houseplant fertilizer at half strength every 3 or 4 weeks. To prevent the plants from flowering and ensure tastier leaves, keep the stems cut back to 13 cm (5 inches). If plants start to yellow, repot into a larger container, or divide the root mass into separate pots.

> *Mentha is said to be named for Minthe, a charming nymph of classical mythology, who caught the fancy of Pluto, god of the underworld. In a fit of jealousy, Prosperina, Pluto's wife, changed Minthe into a humble plant. Taking pity on poor Minthe, Pluto bestowed great fragrance on the plant.*

HARVESTING NOTES
- Pick leaves and stem tips for fresh use at any time once the plants are about 15 cm (6 inches) tall. For best flavor, pick before the plants flower.
- For drying, cut stems to just above the lowest set of leaves. Harvest before flowering, cutting stems in the morning, after the dew dries. Hang leafy stems upside down in small bunches in a shady location to dry. When dry, strip leaves and store in airtight jars in a dark location. Don't crumble leaves until you are ready to use, as their flavor will diminish.
- Freeze leaves in butter, oil, or ice cubes for later use.

The English naturalist John Ray (1627–1705) first gave peppermint its name, although to this day, no one knows why, as the plant does not taste like pepper.

CULINARY USES

- Float fresh mint leaves on cool summer drinks and fruit punches. Mint is as essential for mint julep as bourbon, and is a natural addition to any gin-based drink.
- Enliven salads and hot and cold soups with fresh mint.
- Bring out the flavor of peas, new potatoes, and baby carrots by adding sprigs of fresh mint to the cooking water.
- Use fresh or dried mint to season savory dips, butter, sauces, and jellies, especially the classic mint sauce or mint jelly served with roast lamb.
- Season fish, poultry, and meats with mint, and use it to add zest to bean and lentil-based dishes.
- Unless you're using mint as a garnish, always crush the leaves before use to obtain optimum flavor.

Curly-leaved Spearmint

- Add sprigs of fresh mint to vinegar.
- Brew a soothing cup of mint tea by infusing 5 mL (1 teaspoon) of dried leaves or 15 mL (3 teaspoons) of crushed fresh leaves in 250 mL (1 cup) of boiling water. Steep to taste.
- Mints are used commercially to flavor confectionery, chewing gum, soft drinks, baked goods, ice cream, gelatins, syrups, and liqueurs.

The motion picture character Forrest Gump said, "Life is like a box of chocolates: you never know what you're going to get." Actually, the squiggles on chocolates often indicate the filling: a round chocolate with a circle on top usually has orange filling; an "R" on the top usually means raspberry; a loop down the side of the chocolate generally indicates lemon; a "V" usually stands for vanilla. And, most dependable of all, a straight line means peppermint.

CRAFT USES

- Add aromatic mint leaves to sachets and potpourris.

MEDICINAL USES

- Oil of peppermint was used in traditional folk medicine as an antiseptic, a deodorant, and a stimulant, and to treat a variety of maladies including headache, insomnia, anxiety, pregnancy-related nausea, digestive upsets, bronchitis, asthma, sore throats, cancer, rheumatism, toothache, and neuralgia. Peppermint oil, mixed with salt, was once applied to bites from a rabid dog.
- In modern medicine, peppermint oil has been used to reduce menstrual cramps and stimulate the appetite, and to treat digestive disorders, diarrhea, flatulence, and cholera.
- Peppermint is widely used commercially to disguise the taste of many medicines and to flavor toothpaste and mouthwashes.
- Fresh mints are a source of vitamin C and provitamin A.

In the Middle Ages, fresh mint was put near cheese and stored grain to ward off mice and rats.

CAUTIONS

- Do not give peppermint tea to babies and young children as the menthol may cause asphyxiation.
- Very large consumption of peppermint can aggravate gallstones.
- Unlike many herbal teas, mint teas do contain tannin.
- Pennyroyal mint (*M. pulegium*) contains too much poisonous pulegone to be consumed safely. Pennyroyal flea products are sometimes available to protect pets, but you should not use these dangerous products on your dog or cat.

CULTIVARS AND RELATIVES

There are 19 species of mint, plus 13 hybrid species, and abundant variety within the species, so selecting mints for the herb garden is limited only by personal taste and space availability.

- Peppermint (*M. × piperita*). Easily recognizable spicy peppermint aroma and flavor. Makes an excellent herbal tea and is the culinary herb most used in modern Western medicine. Dark green leaves, which are attached to the plant's stem with leaf stalks, are heavily veined and coarse-textured.
- Spearmint (*M. spicata*). Essential for mint sauce and mint julep and all drinks and dishes that benefit from the zing that only mint can impart. Slightly crinkled leaves, which are attached to the plant's stem without leaf stalks, have a lemon-mint aroma and a distinctive, pungent, camphor-like taste.
- Apple mint (*M. suaveolens*). Round, grayish-green leaves have downy white undersides and a delicate apple aroma. A delightful tea herb.
- Variegated ginger mint (*M. × cardiaca* 'Variegata'). Very pretty, golden variegated leaves combine mint with a mild ginger flavor and an agreeable fruity fragrance. Adds life to green salads.
- Variegated pineapple mint (*M. suaveolens* 'Variegata'). Often grown as an ornamental for its beautiful, apple green, woolly, rounded leaves that are flecked and bordered with creamy white. Has a sweet, fruity scent. Young leaves have a distinctive pineapple-like fragrance and flavor, which becomes more mint-like as the plant matures.
- Orange mint (*M. × piperita* 'Citrata'). Also known as lemon mint, eau de cologne mint, and bergamot mint. Has large leaves edged with dainty red lines. Bewitching fragrance entices with a hint of citrus. Perfect for summer coolers and teas. Ideal for potpourris and sachets.
- Water mint (*M. aquatica*). Requires wet soil. Round green leaves with a touch of purple have a true menthol flavor and fragrance. Often used to season Southeast Asian meat dishes.
- Corsican mint (*M. requienii*). Attractive, low, ground-hugging plant with tiny, bright green, fragrant leaves is the most delicate mint. Not winter hardy, although it has been known to survive in zone 4 if protected by a mulch of evergreen boughs.

In the classical world, the aroma of mint symbolized hospitality, so Greek and Roman hosts always made sure that table surfaces were rubbed with crushed mint leaves. And at the end of a feast, guests would be offered a sprig of stomach-soothing mint, the forerunner of today's after-dinner mint.

A Potpourri of Mint-Like Herbs

CALAMINT, LARGE-FLOWERED
Calamintha grandiflora
Labiatae (Lamiaceae; mint family)

Zone **5** Coldest Tolerated

Native to southern and south-eastern Europe, Anatolia, and northern Iran. Hardy, erect, aromatic perennial grows from 20 to 60 cm (8 to 24 inches) tall. Woody at the base, with square, downy stems, and soft, light green, stalked, serrated leaves. In midsummer, produces spikes of lovely bright pink, tubular flowers that are attractive to bees. Plant has a strong, penetrating, agreeably fruity aroma, with an overtone of thyme. Grows best in well-drained, relatively alkaline soil. Prefers sunny location, but tolerates partial shade. Propagated from seeds, and by dividing established clumps. Leaves make a delightful, sweet, aromatic herb tea, and are a flavorful substitute whenever mint is called for. *Calamintha* comes from the Greek *kallis*, meaning "beautiful," and *mintha*, "mint," an apt name for a very pretty plant.

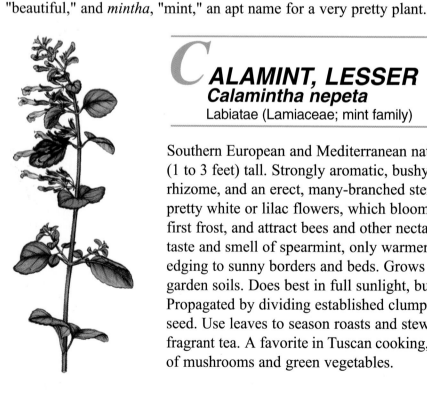

CALAMINT, LESSER
Calamintha nepeta
Labiatae (Lamiaceae; mint family)

Zone **4** Coldest Tolerated

Southern European and Mediterranean native grows from 30 to 90 cm (1 to 3 feet) tall. Strongly aromatic, bushy plant has a long, creeping rhizome, and an erect, many-branched stem. Grayish foliage offsets pretty white or lilac flowers, which bloom from midsummer up to first frost, and attract bees and other nectar-seeking insects. Leaves taste and smell of spearmint, only warmer. Makes a very attractive edging to sunny borders and beds. Grows well in most well-drained garden soils. Does best in full sunlight, but will tolerate slight shade. Propagated by dividing established clumps, by stem cuttings, or from seed. Use leaves to season roasts and stews, and to brew a sweet, fragrant tea. A favorite in Tuscan cooking, especially in the preparation of mushrooms and green vegetables.

KOREAN MINT
Agastache rugosa
Labiatae (Lamiaceae; mint family)

Native to parts of eastern Asia, including India, eastern China, Japan, and Indo-China. Herbaceous, bushy perennial (cultivated as an annual in colder areas) grows to 120 cm (4 feet) tall. Rough, bright green, heart-shaped, serrated leaves have an anise-like flavor and aroma. In late summer, produces purple or rose-violet flowers that are very popular with honeybees. Grows best in well-drained, fertile soils containing well-rotted manure or compost. Requires sunny location. Propagated from seeds. Use leaves to season meats and dressings, and in any recipe calling for mint. Makes an excellent tea. Much used in Chinese herbal medicine.

MEXICAN MINT MARIGOLD
Tagetes lucida
Compositae (Asteraceae; sunflower family)

Mexican and Guatemalan native grows from 30 to 80 cm (1 to 2½ feet) tall. Sparingly branched plant with glossy, lance-shaped leaves and a somewhat woody base. In late summer, produces a cluster of golden-yellow flower heads. Requires loose, well-drained soil. Needs full sun. Propagated from seeds. Anise-scented leaves make a pleasantly sweet and refreshing tea, and are often used in fruit punch, sangría, and cider. Use leaves to flavor vinaigrettes, sauces, and butter, and to complement salads, egg dishes, fish, and poultry. The Aztecs used to add powdered Mexican mint marigold to *chocolatl*, a foaming drink made from cocoa beans.

MOUNTAIN MINT
Pycnanthemum pilosum
Labiatae (Lamiaceae; mint family)

Zone
4
Coldest
Tolerated

North American native grows from 90 to 150 cm (3 to 5 feet) tall. Branching stems, some with clusters of small pink flowers. Dark green leaves produce a pungent, mint-like aroma when crushed. Grows best in rich, well-drained, loamy compost. Keep soil moist. Prefers partial shade, but will grow in full sun. Propagated from seeds or by division. Fresh and dried leaves make a delicious, minty tea. Once prized by North American Indian tribes who used the flower buds as tenderizers for buffalo meat.

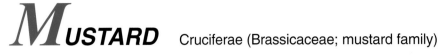

MUSTARD Cruciferae (Brassicaceae; mustard family)

WHITE MUSTARD
Sinapis alba
Also known as: Yellow mustard

Annual

BROWN MUSTARD
Brassica juncea
Also known as: Chinese mustard, Indian mustard, Oriental mustard, Russian mustard, sarepta mustard

Annual

DESCRIPTION

- Mustards have been cultivated for their seeds for over 5 000 years. White mustard is a native of the Mediterranean, central Asia, and North Africa. Brown mustard originated in Asia. Mustards, which are annuals, generally grow from 60 to 120 cm (2 to 4 feet) tall. Both mustards also grow in the wild as weeds.
- White and brown mustard are seed mustards, and should not be confused with vegetable mustards, such as mustard greens. Although seed mustard leaves are edible, vegetable mustards have a superior taste.
- Both mustards have pungent-flavored, broad, dark green, deeply cut lower leaves. Upper leaves are much less dissected, especially in brown mustard.
- Stem and branches are usually hairy in white mustard, slightly hairy in brown mustard.
- Both mustards produce loose clusters of yellow flowers, beginning about 5 to 6 weeks after the seedlings emerge. White mustard flowers are somewhat larger than those of brown mustard.
- White mustard seed pods stand out from the stem and have a long, beak-like tip. Brown mustard seed pods, which form closely to the plant's stem, have a plump, cylinder-like shape when ripe.
- White mustard seeds are white or yellow, odorless, and have a milder flavor than brown mustard seeds. Brown mustard seeds are brown or yellow, and give off a distinctly irritating odor when crushed.
- Leaves, flowers, and seeds of both mustards may be eaten.

White mustard

There are mustards to suit all tastes and complement most savory dishes. Dijon mustard, the French classic, is prepared with brown mustard seeds, water, white wine, salt, and spices. Good Dijon mustard should be light in color, because the seed coat has been removed, sharp, salty, with a true mustard taste. Bordeaux mustard is slightly sweet, darker, and milder than Dijon, with a fine tarragon flavor. Champsac mustard is a dark brown, aromatic, smooth blend flavored with fennel seeds. Champagne mustard is smooth, pale, mild, and blended with champagne. Beaujolais mustard is a blend of coarse-ground seeds and red wine. Red mustard is prepared with chili. Whole grain mustard is a hot, crunchy, English preparation of whole mustard seeds. Honey mustard is a sweet blend of mustard seeds, honey, raw sugar, vinegar, and spices. French herb mustard is usually smooth, mild, and lightly flavored with mixed herbs. German mustard is frequently flavored with herbs and spices, and tends to be somewhat sweet.

CULTIVATION NOTES

- Mustards grow best in well-aerated, loamy soil that is not prone to crusting. Recommended pH range for white mustard is 7.1 to 8.5; for brown mustard, pH should be near neutral, that is, 7.0.
- Mustards prefer full sun. Keep plants moist throughout the growing season.
- Grow both types from seed, which should be planted outdoors early in the spring. Early planting reduces the risk of fall frost damage to the ripening seed pods. Sow seeds to a depth of 6 mm (¼ inch). Seedlings usually appear in 4 to 5 days.
- Space mustards 15 cm (6 inches) apart.
- Keep the ground free of weeds, especially when the seedlings are small. Once established, the plants grow rapidly, shading out weeds.

- Both mustards are susceptible to various fungus diseases and insects, particularly flea beetles. To avoid pests, don't grow mustards or cole crops in the same place for several years. Mustards should not be grown near beets because they host the sugar beet nematode.
- Mustard and cress seed can be germinated together in flats, and the seedlings harvested for mustard and cress sprouts for salads and sandwiches. If you sow mustard 3 to 4 days after cress, both will be ready for harvest at the same time.

Although mustard is cultivated in many countries, Canada is the world's major producer of mustard seed, and is the chief supplier of mustard seed to the United States.

HARVESTING NOTES

- Pick mustard leaves for fresh use when they are young and tender, and not unpleasantly hot to taste. Pick flowers as needed.
- Start harvesting seed pods as soon as they drop their seeds.
- Pick seed stalks and spread them out on a plastic or cotton sheet to dry, preferably in the sun. Flail dried stalks with a broom or baseball bat. Winnow the mixture of stalks, broken pods, and seeds by sifting it slowly through your fingers. While winnowing, hold your hands as high as possible above a bucket, leaving sufficient space between your fingers and the bucket so that the breeze (or an electric fan) blows away the chaff. Repeat sifting until the seeds are clean. Store seeds in an airtight container.

The word "mustard" and its French equivalent moutarde are believed to be derived from the Latin mustum ardens, meaning "burning must," a reference to the ancient Roman practice of beating the seeds in a solution of grape must (unfermented grape juice) to produce a burning heat.

CULINARY USES

- Enliven salads and stir-fry dishes by adding mustard leaves.
- Cook fresh flowers for 3 minutes in boiling salted water. Drain, let stand for a few minutes, and serve with butter.
- Use fresh flowers to make an attractive edible garnish.
- Include whole mustard seeds in pickles, relishes, curries, sauces, and to add flavor to pot roasts and other meats such as lamb, pork, and rabbit. Mustard seeds are essential in sauerkraut, and when cooking strongly flavored vegetables such as cabbage.
- Grind the seeds to form the basis of prepared mustard or mustard paste. Use a food processor, or a mortar and pestle, or place the seeds between 2 sheets of paper and grind them down with a bottle. Ground mustard seeds keep indefinitely.
- Mustard seeds are used commercially in pickling spice mixes, powdered mustard, and in prepared mustards ranging from the ubiquitous bright yellow condiment that is the staple of the fast-food industry to the delectably varied herb- and wine-flavored mustards beloved of gourmets.

In the 13th century, the Earl of Conway executed Vikings who had attacked the Isle of Man by drowning them, upside down, in a barrel of mustard.

MEDICINAL USES

- Mustards have been used in traditional folk medicine as a stimulant, diuretic, and purgative, and to treat a variety of ailments including peritonitis and neuralgia.

- Mustards are still used today in mustard plasters to treat rheumatism, arthritis, chest congestion, aching back, and sore muscles. To make a mustard plaster, mix equal parts of flour and powdered mustard and spread it as a paste on a doubled piece of soft cloth. Apply mustard plaster to the affected area for a maximum of 15 minutes.
- In Chinese herbal medicine, an infusion of mustard leaves is used to treat bladder inflammations and to stop hemorrhage, while the seeds are used to treat abscesses, bronchitis, colds, rheumatism, toothache, ulcers, and stomach disorders.

> *In 1634, the mustard and vinegar makers of Dijon, France, were granted the exclusive right to make mustard in return for wearing "clean and sober clothes."*

CAUTIONS

- As a mustard plaster produces sufficient heat to burn the skin, it must be removed after 15 minutes. Prolonged application can result in burns to the skin and nerve damage. Fumes from a mustard plaster can cause sneezing, coughing, and asthmatic attacks, as well as eye irritation. Do not apply mustard plasters to children under 6 years of age, or to individuals suffering from kidney disorders.

Brown mustard

> *No doubt because of its medical and culinary attributes, mustard is called "the greatest among herbs" in the Bible.*

_N_ASTURTIUM Tropaeolaceae (nasturtium family)

NASTURTIUM
Tropaeolum majus

Also known as: Climbing nasturtium, canary creeper, cress of Peru, garden nasturtium, Indian cress, tall nasturtium

DWARF NASTURTIUM
Tropaeolum minus

Also known as: Lesser Indian cress, small nasturtium, Tom Thumb nasturtium, Yellow Lark's heels

DESCRIPTION

Dwarf nasturtium

- Nasturtiums are perennials, but these bright cheerful ornamentals are grown as annuals in cooler climates. Climbing nasturtium, a vigorous, scrambling vine that grows to about 3 m (10 feet) tall, makes a pretty trellis plant. It is native to Andean South America, including Ecuador, Peru, and Columbia. Dwarf nasturtium, which originated in northwestern South America, grows about 30 cm (12 inches) high, making it perfect for colorful summer pots and hanging baskets, rock gardens, and as an edging for sunny garden plots.
- Bright green, long-stemmed leaves are veined and round with slightly wavy margins. The size of the leaves in either variety depends on the quality of the soil that the plants are grown in. Very rich soil encourages lush foliage, but the tradeoff is fewer flowers; poor soil results in smaller leaves and more flowers. Nasturtium has a mustard-like aroma and a hot, peppery taste.
- Climbing nasturtium has many spreading, fleshy stems that curl around any object they contact, and a tuberous root.
- Under the right soil conditions, nasturtiums produce masses of vibrantly yellow, orange, red, or creamy white flowers that bloom from summer through fall. The open, funnel-shaped flowers usually have a hollow, tube-like extension, or spur, at the base, and have a similar but somewhat milder taste than the leaves.

- Roundish, green seed pods that appear after flowering is finished have a pungently spicy flavor.
- The characteristics of dwarf nasturtium are similar to those of its taller relative, except that it is low, non-climbing, and has smaller flowers with spotted lower petals. The seed pods are also smaller.
- Leaves, flowers, and seed pods may all be eaten.
- Potted dwarf nasturtium may be grown indoors to provide fresh leaves and flowers during the winter.
- Nasturtium is attractive to hummingbirds.

Carl Linnaeus (1707–1778), the famous Swedish botanist, coined nasturtium's genus name Tropaeolum, from the Latin tropaeum, meaning "trophy," which to the ancient Romans was synonymous with a victory in battle. In classical times, the victors would hang captured helmets and shields from a tree trunk set up on the battlefield. In Linnaeus's day, gardeners grew nasturtium plants up poles. To Linnaeus, the plant's rounded leaves were like battle shields, while the flowers were like spear-pierced, bloody helmets.

CULTIVATION NOTES

- Nasturtium grows best in ordinary garden loam, preferably somewhat sandy. The soil should be fairly moist, but well drained.
- Prefers warm, sunny locations, but will tolerate some shade, although plants will not flower as well.
- Grows readily from seed, which should be started indoors about 4 weeks before your last spring frost date. Seeds germinate in about a week. (To speed up the process, soak the seeds overnight in lukewarm water before planting.) Sow seeds to a depth of about 1 cm (½ inch). Young plants are sensitive to frost and should not be transplanted to the garden until late spring.
- Space plants 15 to 30 cm (6 to 12 inches) apart, depending on the variety.
- Provide climbing varieties with a trellis, pole, or fence for support.
- Trim plants if they become scraggly and remove old flowers to prolong flowering. If you plan on harvesting seed pods, stop deadheading in mid-August.
- Nasturtiums do attract aphids. Try to dislodge these pests with a hard spray of water from the hose. Do not use chemical sprays and washes on plants intended for culinary use. Also susceptible to bacterial wilt and leaf spot.
- Start seeds in late summer or early fall for growing indoors on windowsills in the winter. Indoor plants need at least 4 hours of direct sunlight daily. Keep the soil barely moist, and feed the plants occasionally with liquid fertilizer.

Nasturtium

129

HARVESTING NOTES

- Pick leaves for fresh use at any time. Leaves are most tender before the plants flower.
- To dry nasturtium leaves, chop them into small pieces and place on a cookie sheet in a cool, shady location. Alternatively, dry whole leaves and then crumble them. Store dried leaves in an airtight container.
- Harvest flowers when they are fully open, but still fresh.
- Collect seeds pods when they are small or full size, but still green.

The common name "nasturtium" designates the species of the South American genus Tropaeolum, not the species designated by the scientific name Nasturtium, which refers to vegetable watercress. As nasturtium grew in popularity in European gardens, the name transfer seems to have come about through the similar taste of the leaves, flowers, and seed pods of Nasturtium and Tropaeolum.

CULINARY USES

- Add leaves to green salads and potato salads, and use in sandwiches as a substitute for cress. Stuff the leaves with your favorite meat or cheese fillings. The leaves taste best when eaten fresh, as they are inclined to become rather bitter if kept too long.
- Use leaves to season cheese spreads, salad dressings, and in sauces to accompany asparagus, salmon, and crab dishes.
- Add the lovely flowers to salads, both for color and taste.
- Garnish summer dishes with nasturtium flowers and leaves.
- Pickle the seed pods in wine vinegar for about 4 weeks, and then use as a substitute for capers.

CRAFT USES

- Use cheerful nasturtiums in fresh floral arrangements.

MEDICINAL USES

- In traditional herbal medicine, nasturtium was used to stimulate the appetite, to counteract scurvy, and to treat urinary tract infections, influenza, and skin eruptions. In Europe, nasturtium is still occasionally employed in modern medicine for some of these traditional usages.
- Nasturtium leaves are rich in vitamin C, while the seeds are high in iron and phosphorus.

US President Thomas Jefferson (1743–1826) grew many herbs at Monticello, his well-known estate in Virginia. His favorite herb was nasturtium. But Jefferson was not the only president to appreciate this herb. President Dwight Eisenhower (1890–1969) liked his vegetable soup seasoned with nasturtium.

CAUTIONS

- Mustard oil in nasturtium can be irritating both internally and externally to sensitive individuals, and regular contact with the fresh plant may lead to skin problems.
- Young children and people suffering from gastrointestinal ulcers or kidney diseases should not eat nasturtium.
- Eat pickled nasturtium seeds in moderation as they can have a laxative effect.

OREGANO *Origanum vulgare*
Labiatae (Lamiaceae; mint family)
Also known as: Culinary oregano, true oregano, Turkish oregano, winter marjoram, winter sweet marjoram (erroneously called wild marjoram)

Zone 4 Coldest Tolerated

DESCRIPTION

- The best type of oregano is Greek oregano, which we recommend. This is subspecies *hirtum* of *O. vulgare*, but is sometimes incorrectly called *O. heracleoticum*. Most other types of *O. vulgare* lack the true oregano flavor and don't make good culinary herbs.
- Greek oregano, a half-hardy perennial sometimes cultivated as an annual in cooler climates, grows up to 0.6 m (2 feet) tall. It is the essential ingredient of Italian and Mediterranean cuisine. Oregano grows wild from the Azores, Madeira, and Canary Islands in the eastern Atlantic Ocean, through Europe, west and central Asia, to east Asia and Taiwan.
- Dark green, opposite leaves have smooth edges and are highly aromatic. The earthy flavor is pungent, spicy, and biting, with a tantalizing sweetish undertone.
- Greek oregano has slim, squarish, woody, branched stems that grow in a clump, and a branching taproot.
- Produces spikes of small pink, white, or purplish flowers above the leaves. Blooms in early summer.
- May be grown indoors for winter use.

CULTIVATION NOTES

- Greek oregano grows best in light, rich, well-drained soil. Tolerated pH range is 4.5 to 8.7.
- Requires a warm, sheltered location in full sunlight. Allow top 2.5 cm (1 inch) of soil to dry out between waterings.
- Buy young plants from your nursery for planting in spring or early summer. Although Greek oregano can be cultivated from seed, the flavor and aroma of the resulting plants are usually disappointing.
- Space plants 30 cm (12 inches) apart. Weed regularly, as the plants grow slowly.

131

- Can also be propagated by layering stems from existing plants. In early summer, pin down stems to the ground and cover with soil until they root. Keep soil moist. Transplant new plants in early fall.
- Pinch off flowers as they develop to ensure an ongoing supply of leaves.
- Do not overfertilize, as the result is larger but less tasty plants.
- Susceptible to root rot and leaf spot, and infestations of aphids, spider mites, and leaf miners.
- In fall, pot plants for indoor use in dry, free-draining, sandy soil. Water well, and then let soil dry between waterings. Be careful not to overwater. Place pots on a sunny windowsill, as Greek oregano needs at least 5 hours of direct sunlight daily. Pinch off flower buds to stimulate leaf growth.
- Replace older potted plants, as the flavor diminishes with time.
- Replant indoor plants in the garden in the spring, after all danger of frost is passed.

HARVESTING NOTES
- Pick small sprigs of leaves as needed at any time throughout the growing season.
- Harvest leaves and stems for drying when flowers are blooming, as the flavor is at its peak at this time. Cut stems 2.5 cm (1 inch) from the ground, tie cut plants in bunches, and hang in a warm, dry, shady location. Strip dried leaves and store in an airtight container. Dried leaves are more intensely flavored than fresh leaves.

Prior to World War II, there was little demand for oregano in the United States. Although the country's first pizzeria opened in New York in 1895, the American love affair with pizza owes its beginnings to the Italian campaigns of World War II. While on active service, American soldiers discovered pizza, and brought their craving for it back to America. The resulting post–war pizza craze saw a 6 000 percent increase in the demand of oregano over the next 20 years. For the record, 28.4 g (1 ounce) of oregano will properly season 432 slices of pizza.

CULINARY USES
- The best oregano is said to grow in the wilds of Greece, where it is picked by shepherds; however, you won't be disappointed when you use your homegrown Greek oregano in any recipe calling for the herb, be it pizza, pasta, omelets, tomato dishes, Italian sauces, salads, shellfish, cheese spreads, vegetable casseroles, soups, stews, poultry, and meat dishes featuring pork, beef, lamb, and veal.
- Crush leaves and add to a hot dish only in the last 10 minutes of cooking. Use sparingly.
- Flavor olive oil by adding sprigs of Greek oregano.

MEDICINAL USES
- In traditional herbal medicine, oregano was used to treat headaches, diarrhea, insect bites, toothache, coughs, and other ailments. Although still occasionally employed in herbal medicine, oregano is not used in modern medicine.

Oregano means "joy of the mountain," and comes from the Greek oras, *"mountain," and* ganos, *"joy," a fittingly poetic tribute to the fine sight (and scent) afforded by the plants growing on the hillsides in their native Greece.*

CULTIVARS AND RELATIVES
Nothing causes the culinary herb enthusiast more confusion than oregano, as the term is often used to describe a certain spicy flavor and aroma found in dozens of non-*Origanum* species. However, most species of *Origanum*, regardless of their flavor, are attractive additions to any garden.

- Common oregano (*O. vulgare* subsp. *vulgare*). Hardy perennial grows to 0.6 m (2 feet) tall. Lovely pinkish-purple flower spikes lend grace to fresh floral arrangements, or may be dried and used in wreaths and bouquets.
- Mexican oregano (*Lippia graveolens*). The dominant oregano of Mexico and the southern United States. Grows up to 2.5 m (8 feet) tall. Flavor is somewhat sharper and more pungent than that of Greek oregano. In northern climates, can only be grown as a potted houseplant, which can be placed outside for the summer. Use a freely draining, loam-based potting mix of medium fertility.
- Golden oregano (*O. vulgare* 'Aureum'). Very mild flavor. Pretty golden foliage and compact size make it ideal for rock gardens.
- Italian oregano (*O. × majoricum*). Combines the flavor of marjoram and the hardiness of oregano. Noted for its strong taste. Grow as a potted houseplant that can be placed outside during the warmer months.
- Turkestan oregano (*O. vulgare* subsp. *gracile,* usually mistakenly called *O. tyttanticum* in herb catalogs). Dark leaves and bushy growth, with a distinct pungency and strong culinary flavor. Makes an excellent indoor plant.
- Pot marjoram (*O. onites*). Native to southern Greece, Crete, and Sicily, where the plants develop small leaves during the summer droughts common to their natural habitat, and large ones during the wetter winter months. Delightful peppery flavor and thyme-like aroma. Too tender to grow outdoors in cooler climates, but can be cultivated as an edible houseplant.
- Dittany of Crete (*O. dictamnus*). Low-growing shrub with thick, gray, wooly, round leaves and beautiful chartreuse and pink flowers. Native to Crete and southern Greece, where it is in danger of extinction as a result of overzealous picking and excessive grazing. Aromatic foliage is ideal for salads. Grow as an edible indoor plant, that may be kept outside in the summer.

Dittany of Crete

• Syrian oregano (*O. syriacum*). The ancient "hyssop" of the Bible, Syrian oregano was once an important part of ancient Jewish purification rites. Use leaves and flowering tops for seasoning. Flavor is reminiscent of a blend of thyme, sweet marjoram, and Greek oregano, with its own particular added bite. Too frost-tender for cooler climates, but makes a fine edible indoor plant.

Before foreign perfumes were imported into England, domestic toiletries included powders and washing "waters" made with oregano.

Turkestan oregano

Italian oregano

PARSLEY *Petroselinum crispum*
Umbelliferae (Apiaceae; carrot family)
Also known as: Common parsley, curly parsley, or flat-leaved parsley,
depending on leaf type

Zone **3** Coldest Tolerated

DESCRIPTION

- Parsley, the chef's favorite garnish, is an attractive, hardy biennial or short-lived perennial that is usually grown as an annual. In the first year, curly parsley grows from 24 to 30 cm (10 to 12 inches) tall, while flat-leaved parsley reaches to 45 cm (18 inches) in height. In the second year, the flowering stems reach about 0.6 m (2 feet). Parsley probably originated in southern Europe or western Asia.
- Curly parsley, also known as French parsley, (*P. crispum* var. *crispum*) has finely cut, shiny, rich green, ruffled leaves that grow in tufts at the crown of the branches. The flavor and aroma are spicy yet fresh, with a sweetish undertone.
- Flat-leaved parsley, often called Italian parsley, (*P. crispum* var. *neapolitanum*) has small, celery-like, dark green leaves that are stronger and more complex in taste and aroma than those of curly parsley.
- Parsley has a slightly furrowed, many-branched stem, and thin, fibrous roots. The main taproot penetrates deeply into the ground.
- Produces umbels of little yellowish or white flowers that bloom in early summer of the second year, followed by oval, grayish-brown seeds.
- May be grown in containers or pots, both outside and indoors. (A deep pot is best to accommodate the long taproot.)

Common parsley

CULTIVATION NOTES

- Parsley does best in highly fertile, well-drained soil. Tolerated pH range is 4.9 to 8.2. Keep plants watered during dry periods.

- Thrives in full sun, but will grow in light shade.
- Propagate parsley from seed, even though germination is slow and erratic. To speed up germination, soak the seeds overnight in lukewarm water. (Unfortunately, parsley seeds become adhesive when wet and will stick to your fingers like glue, so wear gloves when planting.) You can also freeze the seeds briefly to help break dormancy.

Common parsley

- Start seeds indoors, about 4 to 6 weeks before your last spring frost date. Plant seeds to a depth of 6 mm (¼ inch). Seedlings usually emerge in 15 to 21 days. Transplant to the garden about a week before your last frost date. (A light frost will not harm the plants.) Be careful not to damage the taproot.
- Alternatively, plant seeds outdoors when the soil can be easily worked in the spring. (Don't sow seeds outdoors too soon, as the plants may bolt prematurely.) If planting directly in the garden, mix in a few radish seeds (which germinate quickly) to help mark the parsley rows.
- Keep the soil moist during germination and early growth.
- Space plants 30 cm (12 inches) apart.
- Susceptible to crown rot, and to occasional infestations of parsleyworms, carrot rust fly, and aphids.
- Plants produce only a rosette of leaves in the first year. For a seed crop, leave the plants in the ground until the second season, when they will flower and set seed.
- Parsley, which is a cool-season plant, self-sows. Once established, a patch can maintain itself as far north as zone 3. (Flat-leaved parsley is hardier than the curly variety.) If you want to harvest seeds from the plant in the second season, mulch lightly to provide winter protection. However, to guarantee a regular harvest, sow seeds every year.
- Pot outdoor plants for indoor use in late summer. To ensure a continuing supply of fresh leaves throughout the winter, indoor plants require at least 5 hours of direct sunlight or 12 hours of artificial light daily. A cool, sunny windowsill is the best location. Water regularly and fertilize every 4 to 6 weeks.

Both the ancient Greeks and Romans used parsley medicinally to strengthen the blood, soothe the stomach, and treat hangovers. As a preventative measure, warriors attending celebratory banquets always wore a parsley wreath, a habit that was copied by Roman civilians.

HARVESTING NOTES

- Harvest the outer leaves for fresh use, drying, or freezing throughout the growing season. If not picked, these leaves become coarse and their flavor diminishes. Gather the leaves early in the morning, when it is still cool.
- To dry, spread leaves on a screen and leave in a shady, well-ventilated spot. Crumble dried leaves and store in an airtight container.
- Alternatively, and preferably, freeze leaves on a cookie sheet, then store in freezer containers. Parsley retains its color and flavor better with freezing than drying.

In the Middle Ages, parsley was believed to be evil because it was considered to be one of the Devil's favorite plants. The only way to overcome the herb's wickedness was to sow it on Good Friday, under a rising moon. The Devil also plays a part in parsley's notoriously slow germination speed, as borne out by the old saying: "Parsley seed goes nine times to the Devil and back before it starts to grow."

CULINARY USES

- Parsley's culinary uses are endless and should not be limited to providing an attractive garnish for savory dishes. Add the leaves to soups, stews, stuffing, sauces, vegetable dishes, eggs, savory pies, and casseroles, and use when preparing meat, fish, and shellfish.
- Include fresh parsley in salads—it's an essential ingredient of tabbouleh, a tasty staple of Middle Eastern cuisine—and in savory mousses, dips, biscuits, and crackers.
- Parsley is a mainstay of fine French cooking. It's included in *bouquet-garni*, along with bay leaf and thyme, in *aux fines herbes*, a mixture of parsley, tarragon, chives, or chervil, and in *persillade*, a finely chopped mixture of parsley and shallots that is traditionally added to a dish just before it has finished cooking.

Curly parsley

- Italian chefs prefer the stronger taste of the flat-leaved variety and use it extensively.
- The oil from parsley leaves and seeds is used commercially to flavor cured and canned meats, condiments, sauces, pickles, baked goods, and soups.

Parsley has long been chewed as an after–dinner breath freshener, especially following meals with considerable onion or garlic. There is no proof that it works.

MEDICINAL USES

- In traditional folk medicine, parsley was held to have many beneficial properties. Bruised leaves were used as a poultice for sore eyes and to treat insect bites and stings, while a dusting of powdered parsley seed was supposed to cure baldness. Nursing mothers were advised to apply the leaves regularly to the breasts to suppress lactation. Parsley juice was a popular general tonic and was believed to be very good for the kidneys. An infusion of parsley was also used to treat asthma, tumors, warts, dysentery, dropsy, fever, jaundice, menstrual difficulties, and urinary disorders.
- Parsley leaf oil, which contains apiol, is being studied to assess its value for treating some digestive and urinary tract problems, but at present it appears to be of minimal use in modern medicine.

- Parsley oil is used commercially in personal care products such as conditioners for dry hair, perfumes, soaps, and creams.
- Parsley is rich in vitamins C and A, iron, iodine, calcium, fiber, riboflavin, thiamine, niacin.

CAUTIONS

- Parsley oil may cause dermatitis in some people. The oil is very toxic and should only be handled by professionals.
- Parsley is occasionally used in large amounts for medicinal purposes. If you are pregnant, you should not take such large amounts, as parsley is a uterine stimulant. Individuals suffering from inflammatory kidney disease should also refrain from using large amounts of parsley.

CULTIVARS AND RELATIVES

- Turnip-rooted parsley or Hamburg parsley (*P. crispum* var. *tuberosum*). Grown as a vegetable for its thick, tapering, off-white, edible root, which can be cooked and served like parsnip, or grated raw into salads. Flavor is reminiscent of carrot and celery, with a mildly nutty overtone. Use leaves as a garnish or in any recipe calling for parsley.
- Dark moss-curled parsley. Very reliable, standard curly variety with bright green, deeply cut leaves.
- Forest green parsley. Leaves are not as deeply cut or curled as dark moss-curled variety. Excellent flavor.

Turnip-rooted parsley

In classical times, parsley was associated with death. It was said to have sprung from the blood of the Greek hero, Archemorus, the forerunner of death, and so was never eaten. Instead, it was used in funeral rites and parsley wreaths were placed on the tombs of the departed.

POPPY, ORIENTAL *Papaver orientale*
Papaveraceae (poppy family)

Zone
3
Coldest
Tolerated

DESCRIPTION

- Oriental poppy, perhaps the most striking of all culinary herbs, is a long-stemmed, hardy perennial that can grow up to 1.5 m (5 feet) tall. Gorgeous to look at and easy to grow, this native of the mountains of Turkey makes a spectacular garden ornamental.
- Oblong, coarse, hairy, bright green leaves, which are about 8 cm (3 inches) long, are opposite and dissected into lobes with serrated margins. After the plants flower, the leaves turn yellow and die down.
- Oriental poppy has tall, stiff, hairy stems with many grooved branches, and a long, easily breakable taproot.

Oriental poppy

- Produces distinctive big buds covered in bristly hairs from which the dramatic flowers in scarlet, pink, orange, white, or coral emerge in late spring. Bowl-shaped, short-lived flowers, which can be 15 cm (6 inches) or more across, have 6 silken-textured, ruffled petals that are marked with black at the base. Still others have colorful stamens at the center.
- Attractive, grayish-green, vase-shaped seed heads form after flowering is finished. Pods contain thousands of tiny, dark brown, kidney-shaped, edible seeds, which have a mildly spicy, oily, agreeably nutty flavor.

CULTIVATION NOTES

- Oriental poppy thrives in light, fast-draining, warm soil that is not strongly acidic. Do not overfertilize.
- Does best in full sun, but will tolerate light shade. Requires extra watering only if the season is particularly dry. Water-logged soil, especially in the winter, will kill the plants.

- Grows readily from seed, which should be sown outdoors in early spring as soon as the ground is workable. Scatter the seeds on the earth's surface and keep well watered until the seedlings appear. Seeds germinate in about 10 to 15 days. Wet, cool weather is ideal after the seeds are sown; however, once the roots are established, the plants prefer hot, dry weather.
- Sow the seeds where you want the plants to grow, as seedlings don't transplant well. When choosing a location, bear in mind that Oriental poppies die back quickly after flowering, so plant them among other perennial herbs or flowering plants that will help hide the gaps. New foliage begins in the fall and continues through the winter.
- May also be propagated from root cuttings, which should be taken once the foliage has died down. Lift the plant and cut the roots into pieces 5 to 8 cm (2 to 3 inches) long. Place the pieces right side up or horizontally in sandy soil, 45 to 60 cm (18 to 24 inches) apart.
- Apart from dividing the plants every 5 years or so, and stalking the tallest varieties, Oriental poppies don't require much attention. Divide the plants in late summer or early fall, when they begin to grow again. Plants may take 2 years to come back into bloom after dividing.
- Clumps of Oriental poppy can become quite large, but they are not invasive.
- Susceptible to downy mildew in damp conditions, and to infestations of black bean aphid and capsid bugs.
- Overwinters outdoors up to zone 3. Mulch new plants during their first winter, applying mulch around the foliage, rather than on top of it.

Poppy seeds are so small that about 20 million of them weigh just 1 kg (2.2 pounds).

HARVESTING NOTES

- Harvest Oriental poppy for seeds when the fruits turn grayish-brown.
- Snap the seed heads off the dried stems straight into a paper bag. Leave the seeds in the open bag to dry in a well-ventilated location. When the seeds are completely dry, close the bag and shake vigorously. Open the bag and sieve contents over a bowl to separate the seeds from the chaff. Collect the seeds and store in an airtight container.

Poppy seeds seem to have been used for culinary purposes since the Neolithic Age, at least 4 000 years ago. In the second millenium BC, the Egyptians cultivated poppy to obtain the edible oil in the seeds, and both the ancient Greeks and Romans used the seeds to flavor bread and cakes. Using poppy seeds on baked goods was a widespread practice by the Middle Ages.

CULINARY USES

- Poppy seeds are at their best when they are baked or steamed and then crushed before using. This process brings out the seeds' delicious nutty flavor and crunchy texture. Baked or steamed seeds can be wrapped in a kitchen towel and then hammered with a rolling pin or wooden mallet. Frequent poppy seed users may want to consider investing in a hand-mill specially designed for grinding the seeds.
- Sprinkle the seeds generously on top of rolls, bagels, bread, and cookies. Use ground poppy seed alone, or with raisins and other ingredients of your choice, as filling for sweet pastries,

such as poppy seed apple strudel and hamantaschen, the delicious triangular-shaped treat always served during the Jewish holiday of Purim. Seeds are the essential ingredient of poppy seed cake and lemon poppy seed muffins, always popular when a not-too-sweet accompaniment for tea or coffee is called for.

- Add zing to noodles, pasta, stews, casseroles, and vegetables such as potatoes and turnip by including poppy seeds, and use seeds to flavor salad dressings, dips, butter, cream cheese, and sour cream.
- In Indian and Iranian cuisine, poppy seedlings are added to soups or cooked and eaten as greens.

MEDICINAL USES

- Oriental poppy is not used medicinally.
- Poppy seeds are rich in carbohydrates and calcium, and are a good source of energy.
- Poppy-seed oil has a very high content of unsaturated fatty acids, especially nutritionally valuable linoleic acid.

CRAFT USES

- Create dramatic fresh floral arrangements with Oriental poppies. To prolong the life of the flowers, cut tight buds early in the morning and sear the cut end of each stem with a match or candle flame before placing it in water. Alternatively, dip the stem ends in boiling water for a few minutes, taking care to protect the flowers from the rising steam.
- Include the arresting seed heads in dried floral arrangements. (Treat the stem ends as above.)

Opium poppy

CULTIVARS AND RELATIVES

- Opium poppy (*P. somniferum*). Because it's the source of opium and the narcotic alkaloids morphine and codeine, it is illegal to cultivate opium poppy in North America. Despite this, opium poppies are commonly grown as garden ornamentals, and are offered in reputable seed catalogs. Most people simply don't realize that the poppy seeds that are widely used on breads and pastries and the ornamental opium poppies grown in gardens come from exactly the same species that is used to produce illicit opium and heroin, as well as licit drugs used to control pain. The laws governing the cultivation of opium poppy, which can lead to long prison sentences if broken, also apply to the cultivation of ornamental opium poppies. It is astonishing that ornamental opium poppies, whose seeds are excellent for culinary use, continue to be offered for sale and are widely grown. Home gardeners should know that if they are discovered cultivating ornamental opium poppies, the plants would have to be destroyed. Ornamental poppies are beautiful culinary herbs that do not deserve to be hunted down like criminals, and we can only hope that common sense will continue to be exercised.
- Corn poppy (*P. rhoeas*). Also known as Shirley poppy, these beautiful annuals grow to about 60 cm (2 feet) tall. Flowers come in shades of red, pink, purple, and white. Seeds have a delectable, mildly nutty flavor.

ROSE — *Rosaceae (rose family)*

DOG ROSE
Rosa canina

Also known as: Briar rose, brier rose, common brier, dog brier, doghip, hip rose, wild dog rose

TURKESTAN ROSE
R. rugosa

Also known as: Japanese rose, large-hip rose, ramanas rose, rugosa rose, wrinkled rose

Zone **3** Coldest Tolerated

Zone **2** Coldest Tolerated

DESCRIPTION

- Roses, the beautiful, fragrant, prickly, usually upright, perennial shrubs cultivated since antiquity, have an equally venerable culinary history. Archaeological evidence indicates that humans intentionally collected rose fruits for food from 5000 BC. Dog rose, which is native to Europe, western Asia, and North Africa, grows to 3 m (10 feet) tall. Turkestan rose is a native of eastern Russia, Korea, northern China and Japan. Perhaps the most ornamental of all the roses, it grows to about 2 m (6½ feet) tall.

- Dog rose has glossy green, oval-shaped, pointed leaves with serrated edges. Turkestan rose has bright green, toothed, alternate, heavily veined leaves that have a distinctive wrinkled (*rugosa* means "wrinkled") appearance.

- Dog rose has arching, thorned stems or canes, while Turkestan rose has erect stems covered with prickles and bristles.

- Dog rose produces fragrant pink or white flowers that bloom from June to July. Equally fragrant Turkestan rose blooms throughout the summer, generally with rose-purple or white flowers that are up to 8 cm (3 inches) across. Flowers of both roses grow singly or in small clusters. Double-flowered forms of Turkestan rose are also available. Rose petals have a delicate, exotic taste.

Dog rose

- Fruits, the so-called rose hips, follow the flowers. Rose hips are actually "false fruits," each containing a number of true fruits. Inside the hips are hairy achenes, a type of fruit with a dry wall and a single seed. Dog rose hips are oval, orange-red or scarlet, and about 1 cm (½ inch) long. Turkestan rose hips are glistening brick-red, sometimes orange, conspicuous, and about 2.5 cm (1 inch) in diameter. Rose hips have a sweet, tangy flavor. Normal flowers with only 5 petals tend to produce the better hips.
- Both petals and hips may be eaten.

> *With imported citrus fruit unobtainable during World War II, beleaguered Britons turned to rose hips to meet their vitamin C requirements. While the British Ministry of Health distributed National Hip Syrup, the German Navy, faced with a similar vitamin C shortage, supplied submarine and ship crews with rose hip syrup.*

CULTIVATION NOTES

- Roses do best in rich, deep loam that both retains moisture and is well drained. (Turkestan rose is rather adaptable and does well in both pure sand and clay.) Roses generally prefer a slightly acidic soil. The recommended pH range is 6 to 6.5.
- Both roses prefer full sunlight, although they will tolerate light shade. Water regularly.
- Roses are propagated from seeds, by cuttings, layering, division, and grafting or budding; however, most of these methods usually require a horticulturist's skill. (Turkestan rose is the exception, as it suckers readily and can be divided quite easily. Divide when you are pruning the plants before they leaf out.) Home gardeners are advised to buy rose bushes in spring from a reliable local nursery or garden catalog.
- When planting roses, be sure to dig a hole wide and deep enough to accommodate the roots. (Rose roots generally split into several main branches.) Add rotted

Turkestan rose

manure or compost and a few handfuls of bone meal to the planting-hole soil. For grafted roses, plant with the bud union just below the soil surface. (Hardy shrub roses are often not grafted, but are on their own roots. However, some shrub roses, especially hybrids, are grafted to a hardy root.) Tamp down soil and water well. Continue watering until the first signs of growth appear. Mulch an area about 30 cm (12 inches) around the bush to keep down weeds and any competing plants, and to promote moisture retention during dry spells.

- Space bushes 0.6 to 1 m (2 to 3 feet) apart.
- Feed after each blooming period has finished and the new growth is beginning for the next one.
- Each spring, cut out dead branch tips and old canes, and fertilize the bed with rotted manure or compost.
- Roses are very susceptible to rust and black spot, an unsightly fungus, and to infestations of aphids, spider mites, and thrips. As a first defense against disease, avoid watering bushes late in the day. If this is not possible, take care not to wet the foliage.
- Unlike most other roses, shrub roses generally require little or no special winter protection. However, many shrub roses are hybrids, and not as winter-hardy as the species described here. You'll need to protect your hybrids with straw mulch, especially if you garden in a very cold region. Turkestan rose, probably the toughest of all roses, can overwinter out-doors up to zone 2; the less hardy dog rose up to zone 3.

The name "dog rose" is thought to stem from the ancient belief that the plant's root would cure the bite of a mad dog. It is more likely, however, that the common name is derived from an earlier name, "dagger rose," a reference to the plant's formidable thorns. With time, "dag" became corrupted to "dog."

HARVESTING NOTES
- Pick petals before the flowers are fully open. (The darkest petals have the most flavor.) Harvest the flowers on a dry day, before it becomes too sunny. Pull off the petals gently, discarding the green or white heel attached to the flower base. Wash petals and dry them between paper towels. Use immediately.
- Pick petals for potpourris on a sunny day, after the dew has dried. To dry, spread petals on screens in a shady, airy location, or leave them overnight on cookie trays in a just-warm oven. Petals are ready for storage when they are crispy dry.
- Gather rose hips after the first light frost when they are plump and red and just slightly soft to the touch.
- Process harvested rose hips quickly to prevent loss of vitamin C. Trim the stem and blossom ends and cut the hips in half lengthwise. Scoop out the seeds and fibers with a small spoon. Dry the halves on a screen in an airy, shaded, indoor location. Alternatively, dry the hips with hot air from an electric heater. Be careful not to overheat the hips or they will lose color. Shake hips well in a wire sieve to remove hairs. Store in a cool place. Don't keep rose hips for more than a year, as their vitamin C content decreases over time.

Bears are said to relish rose hips as pre–hibernation food.

CULINARY USES

- Use fresh rose petals to garnish salads and fruit plates, and add to cream cheese spreads for bagels and sandwiches. Flavor butter with rose petals, and include the petals in scrambled eggs. Rose petals are often made into jam, jelly, and syrup, and can be crystallized to make attractive decorations for cakes and desserts.
- Steep fresh rose petals in white vinegar.
- To make rose petal tea, infuse 5 mL (1 teaspoon) of dried petals in 250 mL (1 cup) of boiling water. Steep to taste. Also makes a refreshing iced tea.
- Use flavorful rose hips to make jam, jelly, wine, purées, and syrups. Providing the cooking process is not too lengthy, rose hips retain their high vitamin C content, so rose hip purée or syrup makes a nutritious addition to desserts.
- Experiment with rose hips in soups and sauces, and in chicken and pasta dishes.
- Rose hip tea is delicious. As dried rose hips are as hard as coffee beans, you'll need to grind them before use. (Soaking dried hips in boiling water softens them.) Use 5 mL (1 teaspoon) of powdered rose hips to 250 mL (1 cup) of boiling water. Steep for about 5 minutes. Sweeten with honey, if desired. Tastes just as good cold as it does hot.
- Rose extracts are used commercially to flavor beverages, candy, ice cream, baked goods, jelly, and gelatin desserts.

CRAFT USES

- Pick fragrant blooms for fresh summer bouquets.
- Include aromatic dried rose petals in potpourris and sachets.

Roses are the most symbolic flowers. The perfect blossom represents love, beauty, youth, perfection, and immortality, while the withering flower reflects the ephemeral nature of youth and beauty. The thorns epitomize the pain of love and guilt. White roses, often associated with the Virgin Mary, mean purity and innocence; red roses are the embodiment of desire, passion, and shame, and of blood and sacrifice. Yellow roses symbolize perfect achievement to some, jealousy to others.

MEDICINAL USES

- In traditional herbal medicine, dog rose hips were used to treat sore throats and bronchial problems, bleeding gums, diarrhea, hemorrhage, fever, and inflammations. Once looked upon as something of a wonder drug, rose hips were also used to treat epilepsy, tuberculosis, goiter, and gout.
- Rose hips are not used in modern medicine.
- Rose hips, especially those of the dog rose, have a much higher vitamin C content than oranges and lemons. Three rose hips can contain as much vitamin C as a whole orange. And the further north the plants are grown, the greater the vitamin C content of the hips. Rose hips also contain large amounts of provitamin A (carotene), plus some B vitamins (riboflavin and folic acid), and vitamins P, K, and E.

CAUTIONS

- Because of the high ascorbic acid content of rose hips, do not use copper, aluminum, or iron cookware or utensils when preparing food or beverages containing hips. Use only stainless steel, wood, plastic, or glass utensils or cookware.
- Do not pick rose hips for culinary use unless you are certain that the bushes have not been sprayed with pesticides.
- Some people may experience contact dermatitis from handling rose bushes. Rose pollen can be an allergen for sensitive individuals.

The first "rosaries" were made out of pounded rose petals, which were then shaped into beads and threaded together.

CULTIVARS AND RELATIVES

Rosa has over 100 species and at least 13 000 identifiable cultivars. While any of the species and cultivars could be considered for culinary purposes, only a few have been. Here are some reliable favorites:

- Apothecary (*R. gallica* 'Officinalis'). One of the oldest roses in cultivation. Possibly introduced to Europe in the 12th century. Low spreading bush, about 90 cm (3 feet) tall. Semi-double, rich crimson flowers bloom in June, and are followed by small, round, red fruits. Petals were once used widely in medicine and perfume. Best rose for potpourris.
- Virginia (*R. virginiana*). North American native grows to 180 cm (6 feet) tall. Each flower consists of fragrant, variably pink petals. Fruits are small, dark red, and grouped in clusters.
- Jens Munk (*R. rugosa* 'Jens Munk'). Grows to 180 cm (6 feet) tall. Produces lots of lovely, fragrant, semi-double, pure pink flowers, followed by abundant crimson hips the size of marbles.

Apothecary rose

- Scabrosa (*R. rugosa* 'Scabrosa'). Handsome shrub grows to 120 cm (4 feet) tall. Pretty, scented, single flowers are blush-pink with cream-colored stamens. Hips are large, orange-red, and plentiful.
- Kazanlik (*R.* × *damascena* var. *trigintipetala*). The main source of Bulgarian attar of roses, the oil that rises to the surface of rose water and is used in perfume. Very fragrant, semi-double, rose-pink flowers are followed by red hips about 2.5 cm (1 inch) in diameter.
- Rubra Plena (*R. rugosa* 'Rubra Plena'). May grow up to 180 cm (6 feet) tall. Semi-double flowers have dark pink petals with a strong clove scent. Reddish-orange hips are large and round.
- Alba Semiplena (*R.* × *alba* 'Semiplena'). Another old favorite known since at least the middle of the 13th century. Produces wonderfully fragrant, semi-double, white flowers, followed by red hips about 2.5 cm (1 inch) in diameter. Overwinters outdoors up to zone 4.

146

ROSEMARY *Rosmarinus officinalis*
Labiatae (Lamiaceae; mint family)
Also known as: Compass plant, compass weed, dew of the sea, incensier, Mary's mantle, polar plant

DESCRIPTION
- Rosemary, traditionally the herb of friendship and remembrance, is a sweet-scented, shrubby, evergreen perennial that is usually grown as an annual in cooler climates. It is native to southern Europe, Morocco, and Tunisia. Mature plants, which can live for over 30 years, grow from 1 to 2 m (3 to 6 feet) tall.
- Narrow, needle-like, opposite, stalkless leaves are turned at the edges, with a slightly glossy surface and a downy underside. The leaves give off a pungent fragrance rather similar to tea or a combination of pine and nutmeg. The flavor is somewhat peppery, warm, spicy, and resinous, with just a hint of bitterness.
- Rosemary has a somewhat twisted stem with many slender branches, and a taproot.
- Produces pretty pale blue or bluish-lilac flowers (occasionally white or pink) that grow in clusters on the branches. Rosemary usually blooms in late winter or early spring; however, it may fail to flower when grown in more northerly regions.
- Can be grown in containers and pots, both outside and indoors.
- Flowers are very alluring to bees.
- Leaves, stems, and flowers may all be eaten.

CULTIVATION NOTES
- Rosemary grows best in light, well-drained, rather dry soil. Recommended pH range is 6.0 to 7.5. If your soil's pH is below 6.0, add lime or ground-up eggshells. Don't overwater, as very wet soil inhibits growth.
- Prefers full sunlight, but will tolerate semi-shade.
- As rosemary seeds are very slow to germinate and grow, it's best to buy plants.
- If you have access to existing plants, you can also propagate rosemary from stem cuttings. Clip a sprig of new growth, about 15 cm (6 inches) long, from the top of the plant. Strip the leaves from bottom 4 cm (about 1½ inches). Put the bottom of the twig in wet sand to root, which usually takes about 6 weeks. (Adding a rooting hormone will speed up root development.)

- Alternatively, you can propagate rosemary from existing plants by layering. Simply pin down the lower rambling branches of an existing plant to the soil until they root, forming new plants.
- Space garden plants 0.3 to 0.6 m (1 to 2 feet) apart.
- Susceptible to infestations of scale, spider mites, and mealy bugs, and to root rot in soggy soil.
- Although 'Arp,' the hardiest cultivar, has been known to overwinter outdoors up to zone 6, rosemary is best grown in pots and kept indoors during the winter. Grow potted plants in containers that are just large enough for the roots, as rosemary thrives when the roots are somewhat crowded.
- Indoor plants, which do best in a sunny, cool location, need at last 4 hours of direct sunlight or 12 hours of strong artificial light daily. Let the soil become moderately dry between deep waterings. Mist the leaves every second week.
- Use a balanced fertilizer, such as 20–20–20, but don't overfertilize as this reduces flowering, fragrance, and flavor.
- Trim potted plants in the spring before you place them outdoors for the summer. Put pots outside after the danger of frost is passed.
- Replace potted plants every 3 to 4 years, as they are inclined to become straggly.

> *Rosemary originates in the rocky hillsides around the Mediterranean and is well able to withstand the sea's salt spray and fog. Its scientific name Rosmarinus alludes to its origins: ros is the Latin for "dew," and marinus means "belonging to the sea."*

HARVESTING NOTES
- Pick leaves, stems, and flowers for fresh use at any time.
- Harvest leaves and stems for drying just before the plant blooms, as the flavor is at its peak then. Place stems and leaves on a screen to dry in a dark, well-ventilated location. Store dried leaves in an airtight container.
- Freeze sprigs of leaves on a cookie sheet and store in airtight freezer bags for later use.

> *Students in ancient Greece used to braid rosemary wreaths in their hair when taking examinations as the plant was thought to fortify the brain and refresh the memory.*

CULINARY USES
- Fragrant rosemary enhances the flavor of any food – savory or sweet – to which it is added. Widely used to season lamb, pork, rabbit, veal, sausages and stews, as well as chicken, duck, fish, shellfish, egg dishes and pickles, rosemary is also added to jellies, jams, cakes and cookies.
- Add rosemary to salads and vegetable dishes calling for asparagus, broccoli, cauliflower, eggplant, green beans, peas, potatoes, and zucchini.
- Rosemary is an essential ingredient in herb breads and biscuits, including focaccia, the classic Italian flat bread.

- Use rosemary sparingly as the flavor is strong. Soak dried rosemary in hot water before adding it to uncooked foods.
- The flowers, with their milder flavor, can be candied, preserved, or added to jellies, honey, vinegar, and wine.
- Flavor olive oil by adding a few sprigs of rosemary.

The old English saying, "If rosemary prosper, the mistress is master," stems from the belief that a rosemary plant grown outside the home indicates that the wife is the undisputed head of the household.

CRAFT USES
- Include fragrant rosemary in sachets and potpourris.
- Rosemary plants are often used in topiary, that venerable craft in which shrubs are trained into ornamental shapes.

In the Middle Ages, rosemary was believed to grow only in the gardens of the righteous, and so it was used as a magic charm to protect the wearer from the "evil eye." Placing a sprig under your pillow was also believed to have the power to repel evil spirits and bad dreams.

MEDICINAL USES
- In traditional folk medicine, rosemary tea was used to stimulate the heart, alleviate headaches, and induce sleep. It was also employed to treat a wide range of conditions including asthma, baldness, bronchitis, bruises, cancer, chills, colds, coughs, dandruff, fever, hoarseness, hysteria, nervous tension, neuralgia, rheumatism, and sprains.
- Rosemary is not used much in modern medicine, although the oil does have antibacterial properties. Researchers are presently studying the value of rosemary in treating indigestion, rheumatic disorders, and circulatory problems, and there is some promise of new medicinal uses.
- Rosemary oil is used commercially in various personal care products, including shampoos for oily hair and conditioners to bring out the highlights in dark hair.

For centuries, rosemary has been a symbol of happiness, fidelity, and love, and it has long been held that a man indifferent to rosemary's perfume is incapable of truly loving a woman.

CAUTIONS
- Some people may experience dermatitis after using toiletries made with rosemary oil.
- Rosemary was once used to help induce abortions and to stimulate the uterus. It also promotes menstruation, and has been used medicinally to regulate the menstrual cycle. While eating rosemary in the normal amounts used in cooking is generally considered to be safe, if you are pregnant or experiencing menstrual difficulties, you should discuss with your physician just how much rosemary is safe for you to consume.

- Rosemary oil can sometimes be purchased for aromatherapy. This oil should not be taken orally, as it contains camphor as well as other toxic chemicals that can cause epileptic convulsions, digestive difficulties, kidney damage, and even death, if taken in large doses.
- If taken in large amounts, rosemary can stimulate epilepsy, so individuals with this condition should limit their consumption.

> *Legend has it that when the Holy Family was fleeing from Herod's soldiers to Egypt, the Virgin Mary hung her blue cloak one night on a rosemary bush that had white flowers. The next morning the flowers had turned blue, like Mary's garment. From then on, the herb was known as "rose of Mary."*

CULTIVARS AND RELATIVES

While the flavor of all rosemary plants is pretty much the same, the plant's growing habit can be either erect or trailing. The trailing varieties are generally less hardy than the upright.

- 'Arp' (*R. officinalis* 'Arp'). The hardiest upright cultivar of rosemary, it has wintered outdoors, with protection, in zone 6; however, even it is generally grown as an annual in cooler climates.
- 'Majorca' (*R. officinalis* 'Majorca'). Dramatic dark blue flowers and a combined upright and trailing growing habit make 'Majorca' a handsome feature in any herb garden.
- 'Beneden Blue' (*R. officinalis* 'Beneden Blue'). More upright than 'Majorca,' with finer leaves, and bright medium blue flowers.
- 'Blue Boy' (*R. officinalis* 'Blue Boy'). Diminutive variety grows to no more than 0.6 m (2 feet). Perfect for growing indoors.
- Golden Rain rosemary (*R. officinalis* 'Joyce Debaggio'). Excellent flavor. This attractive plant is characterized by the golden streaks that develop along with new growth.
- 'Pink' (*R. officinalis* 'Pink'). Showy upright habit with pretty, aromatic, bright pink flowers.
- 'Pink Majorca' (*R. officinalis* 'Pink Majorca'). Same handsome plant as 'Majorca,' only with lovely pink flowers.

_S_AGE, GARDEN _Salvia officinalis_
Labiatae (Lamiaceae; mint family)
Also known as: Common sage, Dalmatian sage, red sage, true sage

DESCRIPTION

- Garden sage, arguably the world's most popular flavoring and seasoning herb, is native to the Balkan area of the Mediterranean, as well as adjacent parts of the Adriatic Sea. This attractive, aromatic, perennial, somewhat sprawling sub-shrub, which grows from 15 to 75 cm (6 to 30 inches) tall, is also ideal for rock gardens.
- Oblong, grayish-green, woolly, pebbled leaves are about 5 cm (2 inches) long. Some cultivars are variegated with red, yellow, or white. The flavor and aroma are warm, pungent, bitterish, and slightly astringent.
- Garden sage has square, woody, hairy, branched stems, and many-branched roots.
- Produces spires of fragrant flowers in purple or blue, sometimes pink or white, depending on the cultivar. Blooms from late spring to midsummer.
- Flowers are rich in nectar and very attractive to honeybees.

Garden sage

CULTIVATION NOTES

- Garden sage grows best in well-drained, nitrogen-rich clay loam, preferably near a wall so that the plants will be sheltered during harsh winters. Tolerated pH range is 4.9 to 8.2.
- Requires full sunlight for best growth, but will accept light shade. Avoid overwatering, which will stunt growth and may kill the plants.
- Can be propagated by seeds, cuttings, and layering.
- Plant seeds in the garden 2 weeks before your last spring frost date. Sow seeds to a depth of 1 cm (½ inch) or less. Seedlings usually emerge in 14 to 21 days. Thin seedlings to about 0.6 m (2 feet) apart.
- Alternatively, and preferably, if you want particular cultivars, propagate from cuttings, as seeds often don't produce the desired results. Take cuttings in early summer. Clip a sprig of new growth, about 5 cm (2 inches) from the top of the plant. Remove the leaves from the bottom, and put the end of the twig in wet sand to root, usually in 4 to 8 weeks.

151

- Layer branches by bending them over and anchoring a portion under the soil to promote rooting. Expect new roots in about a month.
- Trim back the plants after flowering, and replace them every 3 to 4 years, as they are inclined to become woody and produce poorer quality sage.
- Susceptible to root rot and fungal diseases, and to infestations of slugs and spider mites.
- Overwinters outdoors up to zone 4. To provide winter protection, mulch well with straw or leaves. In regions north of zone 4, cultivate as an annual. (Garden sage does not grow well indoors.)

Salvia comes from the Latin salvere, meaning "to heal" or "to save," and alludes to its use in the ancient world as a medicinal plant. Both the Greeks and the Romans used garden sage as a tonic and as a treatment for snakebite. Drinking sage juice was also said to aid conception—a belief that is totally without foundation!

HARVESTING NOTES
- Pick individual leaves for fresh use as needed.
- Collect young shoots near the tops of the plants for drying just before mature flowers are produced. Tie the shoots in bunches and hang in a warm location to dry. Leaves are fairly thick and dry slowly. Crumble dried leaves and store in an airtight container.
- Freeze sprigs of leaves on a cookie sheet before storing in airtight freezer bags for later use. Alternatively, freeze the leaves in ice cubes. Freezing retains the flavor of garden sage better than drying.
- Stop harvesting in early fall to allow the plants to maintain reserves needed to survive the winter.

CULINARY USES
- Use to season poultry, stuffing, gravies, pickles, soups, and stews. Garden sage aids digestion, so include it when cooking fatty meats such as duck, pork, or sausages. Adding garden sage gives zest to vegetable dishes, especially eggplant, lima beans, and onions, and to omelets, cheeses, tofu, tomato recipes, and cream cheese. But less is more when seasoning with garden sage, as the flavor and aroma can easily overwhelm foods.
- Add ground garden sage to savory biscuits, corn bread, or muffins to serve with chicken or fish, or to accompany a hearty bean or minestrone soup.
- Flavor the cooking oil of your choice by adding garden sage leaves.
- Garden sage is used commercially to season soups, sauces, sausages, preserves, meats, fried chicken, pickles, cheeses, candy, ice cream, chewing gum, baked goods, and vermouth.

The Chinese once valued garden sage so highly that they exchanged 4 kg (almost 9 pounds) of black tea for 1 kg (2.2 pounds) of garden sage from Dutch traders. In England, people used to drink garden sage tea before Chinese black tea became popular.

CRAFT USES

- Fashion dried garden sage branches into herbal wreaths and garlands.

MEDICINAL USES

- In traditional folk medicine, garden sage was used as an astringent, as a tonic to stimulate digestion and cleanse the blood, and as a disinfectant. It was also employed to treat bleeding gums, colds, cancer, diarrhea, upset stomach, excessive perspiration, headaches, measles, mouth ulcers, nervous tension, rheumatism, snakebite, sore throat, toothache, tonsillitis, and venereal disease. As garden sage contains estrogenic substances, sage oil was widely used in herbal medicine to treat female disorders.
- Sage essential oil is used commercially in various personal care products including toothpaste, mouthwash, and deodorant.

> *Garden sage has been grown as a culinary and medicinal plant in central Europe since the Middle Ages. Medieval faith in the curative powers of sage is best expressed by a proverb of the day: "Why should a man die if he has sage in his garden?" Sage was also said to impart wisdom and improve memory, hence a wise person is a "sage."*

CAUTIONS

- Sage contains thujone, a toxic chemical. While the cooking process makes sage safe for culinary purposes, the medicinal use of the plant is questionable. As sage essential oil contains considerable thujone, it should be used only under a physician's guidance. Hot flashes, dizziness, and seizures have been known to occur from prolonged medicinal use of sage essential oil.
- Drinking sage tea to alleviate an upset stomach is probably not a good idea, even though the water used to make the tea will extract only a limited amount of thujone.
- While sage essential oil is used in aromatherapy, some authorities advise against this usage.
- Pregnant women and nursing mothers should not take sage for medicinal purposes as it has a traditional reputation for inducing abortion and drying up the supply of milk.
- Some people may experience contact dermatitis from handling sage.

CULTIVARS AND RELATIVES

Salvia has 900 or more species of annual or biennial herbs, shrubs or sub-shrubs. Any of the following species make flavorful culinary herbs. Several are almost as hardy as garden sage, and can usually overwinter outdoors up to zone 4 as long as they are protected with mulch. Unlike garden sage, these species can also overwinter indoors in pots. Indoor plants need bright light and cool temperatures. Keep the soil slightly dry, but don't let it dry out completely.

- Purple sage (*S. officinalis* 'Purpurascens'). Very fragrant, reddish-purple leaves and cheerful bright blue flowers.
- Golden sage (*S. officinalis* 'Aurea'). Lovely golden yellow and light green variegated leaves. Milder flavor than garden sage.

- Harvest whole stems for drying just before the plants flower. Cut the stems 5 to 8 cm (2 to 3 inches) above the ground.
- Hang stems in bunches to dry in a warm, shady location. When dry, strip the leaves and store in an airtight container.
- Alternatively, wash and dry fresh leaves and freeze them in plastic bags for later use.

The genus name Satureja comes from the Latin satyrus, meaning "a satyr." These mythical creatures, half-man, half-goat, were believed to have acquired their great sexual prowess from eating summer savory, hence the herb's reputation since classical times as an aphrodisiac. Indeed, early herbal guides cautioned against using too much summer savory, especially to season meats, as it was feared that the herb had the power to drive men to unbridled lechery.

CULINARY USES

- Summer savory is widely used to season bean dishes, both because its flavor brings out the good taste of the beans, and because it helps in their digestion. (Summer savory and beans go so well together that many gardeners grow the herb beside their bean rows so that they can be picked together.)
- Use fresh, dried, or frozen leaves to flavor soups and sauces, especially those that are tomato-based, stews, stuffing, gravies, egg dishes, poultry, and chili. Seasoning strong-smelling vegetables such as cabbage, turnips, and Brussels sprouts with summer savory not only enhances their flavor, but also helps diminish the lingering odor. Add summer savory just before the end of the cooking cycle so it does not lose its flavor. When using frozen leaves, double the amount of fresh or dried summer savory specified in your recipe.
- Include fresh or dried summer savory in marinades, and rub meats with fresh leaves prior to cooking.
- Use fresh leaves to enliven salads and season cheese recipes.
- Summer savory is often added to *bouquet garni* and *fines herbes* mixtures. It's also a flavorful substitute for parsley.

CRAFT USES

- Include sprays of pretty summer savory in seasonal bouquets of fresh flowers and add the dried leaves to potpourris.

In Germany and the Netherlands summer savory is so widely used to season bean dishes that its name in each language — Bohnenkraut in German, bonenkruid in Dutch — literally means "bean herb."

MEDICINAL USES

- In traditional herbal medicine, summer savory was used to treat flatulence, liver complaints, and lung ailments, while crushed leaves were applied to bee or wasp stings to bring relief. Summer savory has long been used as a mild antiseptic.
- Chemicals in summer savory's essential oil are known to act against some common food-borne bacteria, so an infusion of summer savory is an old herbal remedy for treating simple diarrhea; however, it's rarely used in modern medicine.
- Summer savory is rich in calcium and vitamin A.

SAVORY, WINTER *Satureja montana*
Labiatae (Lamiaceae; mint family)
Also known as: Savory, Spanish savory, white thyme

DESCRIPTION

- Winter savory, more expansive in habit than summer savory, is a hardy, perennial, dwarf shrub that grows from 15 to 40 cm (6 to 15 inches) tall. It is native to southern Europe, the Ukraine, North Africa, and Turkey.
- Very narrow, dark green, oblong leaves are smooth and shiny. Although many prefer the taste of summer savory, the flavor and aroma of the two herbs are similar, but winter savory is stronger and more piquant, with a heartiness that's reminiscent of sage or thyme.
- Winter savory has erect, woody stems. The root is branched and relatively shallow.
- Produces spikes of small pale lavender or white flowers in early summer.
- May be grown in containers or pots, both outdoors and indoors.
- Both leaves and flowering tops may be eaten.

CULTIVATION NOTES

- Winter savory prefers light, sandy, well-drained soil. Apply compost no more than once every couple of years. Tolerates dry periods. Recommended pH range is 6.5 to 7.3.
- Does best in sunny locations, but will grow in light shade.
- May be cultivated from seed, although germination is slow and uncertain. Start seeds indoors about 10 weeks before your last spring frost date. Plant seeds to a depth of no more than 6 mm (¼ inch). Provide seeds with plenty of light to promote germination. Alternatively, and preferably, buy winter savory plants from your nursery for transplanting in spring or early summer.
- You can also propagate winter savory by dividing existing plants in the spring, rooting softwood cuttings in the summer, or layering the branches in late spring to early summer. (To layer, bend lower branches down to the ground and cover them with soil. Once a layered branch has rooted, remove it from the main plant.)
- Space plants 30 cm (12 inches) apart.
- To maintain good growth, remove dead wood and divide and replant winter savory every 2 to 3 years. In fall, clip plants back to about 15 cm (6 inches) above the ground.
- Usually pest-free, but susceptible to root rot and winterkill if the soil is too rich or too moist.
- Overwinters outdoors up to zone 4. Mulch well with straw or leaves to provide winter protection.

- Pot outdoor plants for indoor use by late summer. Cut mature plants back to half their size, and allow them to recover for 2 to 3 weeks outside before bringing them indoors. Once indoors, plants need a minimum of 5 hours of direct sunlight each day. Let the soil become moderately dry between waterings. Feed plants an all-purpose fertilizer at half-strength every 3 to 4 weeks.

> *In Provence, winter savory is known as* poivre d'âne, *meaning "donkey pepper,"*
> *in recognition of its peppery tang.*

HARVESTING NOTES
- Pick tender branch tips for fresh use as required before the plants flower.
- To dry winter savory, cut stems 20 cm (8 inches) from the base of the plant and hang upside down in a cool, shady location. When dry, crumble leaves and store in an airtight container. Again, harvest before the plants flower, ideally in the morning after the dew evaporates.
- Harvest judiciously as winter savory recovers more slowly from pruning than summer savory.
- Freeze sprigs of winter savory for later use as required.

CULINARY USES
- Use the leaves and flowering tops to season hearty casseroles, soups, stews, and bean and lentil dishes. Winter savory is generally considered too strong for poultry, but it's perfect with red meats and in meat pies, meat loaf, hamburgers, sausages, stuffing, pâtés, marinades, and pickles.
- Use winter savory to season seafood, especially trout, swordfish, or crab, and experiment with it in your favorite egg dishes. A little goes a long way, so add sparingly.
- Winter savory oil is used commercially to flavor condiments, relishes, soups, sauces, sausages, and prepared meats, while the dried leaves are used in vermouth and bitters.

MEDICINAL USES
- In traditional herbal medicine, winter savory was used as a laxative, sedative, stimulant, tonic, vermifuge, and as a treatment for flatulence.
- Winter savory is not used in modern medicine.

> *The verdict is still out on winter savory's efficacy as an aphrodisiac. While some*
> *European herbalists have long championed the use of winter savory massage*
> *cream to stimulate a waning libido, especially in women, the herb's detractors*
> *maintain winter savory actually causes a decreasing interest in sex.*

CULTIVARS AND RELATIVES
- Dwarf winter savory (*S. montana* 'Pygmaea'). Ideal for rock gardens and borders, as it grows no more than 10 cm (4 inches) tall.

SORREL   Polygonaceae (buckwheat family)

GARDEN SORREL
Rumex acetosa

Also known as: Broad-leaved sorrel, common sorrel, cuckoo sorrow, English sorrel, green sorrel, kitchen sorrel, meadow sorrel, sour dock, wild sorrel

Zone 3 Coldest Tolerated

FRENCH SORREL
R. scutatus

Also known as: Buckler-leaved sorrel, round-leaved sorrel, sour grass

Zone 3 Coldest Tolerated

DESCRIPTION

- Garden sorrel, a popular culinary herb in the ancient world and a salad and vegetable plant in the West since the 14th century, is a bushy perennial that grows from 30 to 150 cm (1 to 5 feet) tall. French sorrel, used in France's kitchens since the beginning of that country's recorded history, is a low-growing perennial about 45 cm (18 inches) tall, although it can be as much as 60 cm (2 feet) wide. Garden sorrel is a native of Europe and Asia; French sorrel is native to the mountains of southern and central Europe and southwest Asia.
- Garden sorrel has large, narrow, arrow-shaped green leaves that grow out from a thick basal cluster and are tinged with red when young. Leaves have a distinctive sharp, somewhat bitter, spinach-like flavor, with a tart citrus tang, the result of their high oxalic acid content. French sorrel has green, shield-shaped leaves that are more succulent and sharply acidic than those of garden sorrel, and have a pronounced lemon taste.
- Garden sorrel has an erect, many-branched stem, and deep roots. French sorrel has either prostrate or ascending stems that form thick clumps, and a tough, branched rootstock.
- Garden sorrel produces small reddish-green flowers. French sorrel produces small, green flowers, which turn reddish-brown later. In garden sorrel there are both male plants and female plants. Plants of French sorrel normally have flowers representing both sexes. Both sorrels bloom by midsummer.
- French sorrel may be grown indoors for winter use.

Garden sorrel

CULTIVATION NOTES

- Both sorrels do best in deep, rich, moist but well-drained soil. The sorrels are fairly tolerant of a wide range of soil pH, although garden sorrel prefers acidic soils.
- Both sorrels prefer full sunlight, but will tolerate partial shade. French sorrel is more drought-tolerant than garden sorrel.
- Garden sorrel likes cooler temperatures. Hot weather increases the acidity of the leaves.
- Grow both sorrels from seed, which should be planted directly in the garden in fall or early spring. Plant seeds 6 mm (¼ inch) deep.
- Space seedlings 30 cm (12 inches) apart.
- Garden sorrel can also be propagated by root division; French sorrel by dividing well-grown clumps every third or fourth year.
- Once established, garden sorrel tends to self-sow. As a couple of plants are usually sufficient for most home gardens, cull those you don't want.
- Remove flower stalks of both sorrels to prevent plants from going to seed and to encourage tender new leaf growth.
- Replace garden sorrel plants every 3 or 4 years, as they are inclined to become woody.
- Sorrels are usually disease-free, but are susceptible to infestations of slugs.
- Both sorrels overwinter outdoors up to zone 3.
- Indoor French sorrel plants need at least 5 hours of strong direct sunlight daily. To accommodate its long roots, pot in a deep container of commercial potting soil. Feed with half-strength liquid fertilizer every 2 weeks.

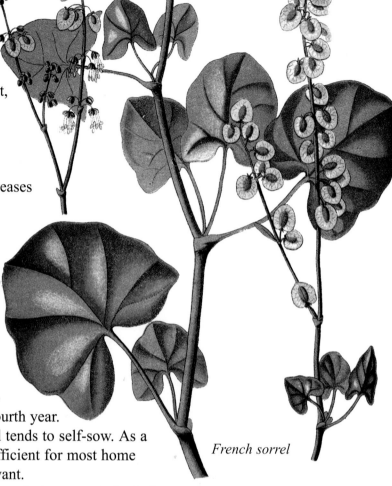

French sorrel

HARVESTING NOTES

- Harvest garden sorrel for fresh use throughout the growing season. If you prefer a more piquantly sour taste, hold off collecting the leaves until the plants are well into the growing season, at which point the flavor is fully developed.

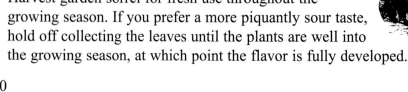

French sorrel

- Begin gathering French sorrel leaves for fresh use from newly sown plants about 2 months after planting. With such young plants, you can gather the shoots whole. As the plants grow, harvest individual leaves rather than whole stalks.
- To preserve sorrel, wash and dry leaves, wrap in a sheet of paper towel, and refrigerate in a plastic bag. Although sorrels wilt quickly after picking, even wilted sorrel retains much of its distinctive taste.
- To dry sorrel, lay leaves out flat in a dark, cool, dry place with good air circulation. Crush dried leaves and store in an airtight container.
- To freeze both sorrels, wash and dry young leaves, wrap in foil, and place in freezer, or purée leaves and freeze in ice cube trays.
- Cut flowering garden sorrel stalks for use in floral arrangements when the flowers are just turning red.

> *French chefs stuff shad with purée of sorrel not only to enhance the flavor of the fish, but also because the oxalic acid softens and partially dissolves the numerous bones.*

CULINARY USES

- Sorrel is often used in French cooking, and is the main ingredient of such culinary classics as sorrel soup and *soupe aux herbes*. (Purists insist that only French sorrel may be used to make sorrel soup, but if you're just becoming acquainted with sorrel, you'd do well to substitute the milder garden sorrel.)

Garden sorrel

- Add sorrel to your favorite spinach and chard recipes, and use it in omelets and soufflés, and in sauces, especially those accompanying, lamb, veal, pork, duck, goose, fish, and shellfish dishes. Sorrel is a tangy addition to early spring salads and mixed green salads. Whatever your recipe, use either sorrel sparingly, tasting as you go, as the sharp flavor does take getting used to.

> *"Sorrel" comes from the Old French* surele, *via the Germanic* sur, *meaning "sour."*
> *In recognition of its acidic taste, English gardeners often called sorrel "sourgrass."*

CRAFT USES

- Include dried garden sorrel blooms in floral arrangements and bouquets.

MEDICINAL USES

- In traditional folk medicine, garden sorrel was used as an antiseptic. Because of its high vitamin C content, it was (correctly) believed to prevent scurvy. Roots and seeds were prescribed as a general tonic, and were used to treat diarrhea, a valid use because of the high tannin content. French sorrel was also used to cure scurvy, cleanse the blood, and promote urine flow. Sorrel was used externally to cure skin disorders and promote a clear complexion.

- Sorrel is not used in modern medicine.
- In addition to being rich in vitamin C, both sorrels are high in vitamin A, and are a good source of iron. French sorrel is also an excellent source of fiber.

CAUTIONS

- Garden and French sorrel should be consumed in moderation, as both are high in oxalic acid, which can cause kidney stones in some individuals. If you are prone to hyperacidity, you probably should avoid sorrel as its high acidity may cause gastric upset. If you suffer from gout or kidney stones, or if you have a history of kidney disease, you should not consume sorrel. Some authorities have also recommended that people afflicted with arthritis or rheumatism should avoid eating sorrel.
- Don't cook sorrel in cast iron pots as the oxalic acid in the leaves will react with the metal, and the leaves will have an unpleasant metallic taste. Also avoid using aluminum cookware, as the oxalic acid could free toxic amounts of aluminum ions. Use stainless steel utensils and cookware when preparing sorrel.
- Avoid sorrel tea because of the oxalates and also because sorrel acts as a diuretic.

Garden sorrel

TARRAGON, FRENCH *Artemisia dracunculus*
Compositae
(Asteraceae; sunflower family)
Also known as: True tarragon, estragon, dragon sagewort, German tarragon

DESCRIPTION

* French tarragon is an exceptionally tasty form of *Artemisia dracunculus*, a wild species native to southeastern Russia, Afghanistan, and western North America. Long a favorite of French chefs, this large, shrubby, highly aromatic perennial grows from 60 to 120 cm (2 to 4 feet) tall. (Wild forms of the species are generally called Russian tarragon. While Russian tarragon seeds are available, the plants produced lack the flavor and fragrance of French tarragon, and are not recommended for culinary use.)
* Dark, shiny, narrow gray-green leaves have smooth edges and grow to about 8 cm (3 inches) long. The distinctive flavor and aroma of the leaves is enticingly bittersweet and anise-like.
* Tarragon has a many-branched, rather woody stem, and a long, brownish root that is gnarled and fibrous.
* Produces loose clusters of tiny yellow flowers in midsummer.
* May be grown indoors for winter use.

CULTIVATION NOTES

* French tarragon grows best in warm, dry, well-drained, light soils. Apply light layer of compost to the soil in early spring. Recommended pH range is 6.0 to 7.5.
* Prefers full sun, but will tolerate filtered sun.
* Propagate by cuttings or by root division, as the seeds are usually sterile.
* Buy young plants from your nursery or garden catalog for planting in spring or early summer.
* Space plants 45 cm (18 inches) apart.
* To keep the roots from becoming entangled, divide established plants each spring just as the first tips of the new shoots are emerging. Pry the plant out of the ground, then use a knife to split the spaghetti-like runners into 3 to 5 shoot divisions. Don't attempt to chop through the roots with a shovel as the new runners are very brittle and break off easily.
* Replace existing plants every 3 to 4 years, as older plants are less flavorful.
* Usually pest-free, but susceptible to root rot in soggy soil.

- Tarragon is reasonably hardy, and should overwinter outdoors up to zone 4. To provide winter protection, cut the stems back before the ground freezes and mulch well with straw or leaves.
- Pot outdoor plants for indoor use by midsummer. The plants should be exposed to cold – at least a month at 4°C (39°F) – before being brought inside, otherwise they may grow poorly. Indoor plants require at least 5 hours of direct sunlight each day, and should be watered only once or twice a week.

> *The genus name Artemisia is said to be derived from Artemis, the name of the Greek goddess of the moon and of hunting, chastity, and childbirth. Another interpretation is that the genus commemorates Artemisia, the wife and sister of Mausolus, King of Caria (in present–day Turkey). When Mausolus died in 352 BC, Artemisia built a magnificent tomb, the Mausoleum, in his honor. The Tomb of Mausolus was one of the Seven Wonders of the Ancient World.*

HARVESTING NOTES

- For best flavor, pick leaves just prior to use.
- To dry tarragon, cut whole branches and hang them in a dark airy location, or strip the leaves off the branches and place on cookie sheets to dry. Crumble dry leaves and store in an airtight container.
- Freezing preserves tarragon's flavor better than drying. Simply freeze leaves in ice cubes, oil, or butter.

CULINARY USES

- Tarragon is essential in the making of Béarnaise sauce, hollandaise sauce, Montpellier butter, sauce tartare, salad dressings and vinaigrettes. It is always included in French *fines herbes* mixtures.
- Use tarragon leaves to flavor fish, shellfish, poultry, meat dishes, particularly veal, creamy soups, omelets, quiche, and delectable *oeufs en gelée*, as well as spinach and mushroom dishes. As it takes but a few minutes' cooking time to release tarragon's flavor, add the leaves when your dish is just about ready to serve.
- Highlight the flavor of steamed vegetables such as potatoes, cauliflower, summer squash, zucchini, and peas by seasoning them with tarragon butter.
- Sprinkle a little fresh tarragon on a green salad. The taste is quite distinct, so use it sparingly.
- Make tarragon vinegar by adding sprigs of fresh tarragon to a bottle of cider, wine, or white vinegar. Leave to steep, in the sun if possible, for 3 to 4 weeks before using.
- Tarragon is the special ingredient in certain French Dijon mustards. It's used commercially to flavor beverages, baked goods, vinegar, mustard and other condiments, salad dressings, sauces, and soup mixes.

> *In the Middle Ages, tarragon was said to increase physical stamina, so pilgrims put sprigs of the herb in their shoes to give them strength to complete their travels.*

MEDICINAL USES

- In traditional folk medicine, tarragon was used as a breath sweetener, as a poultice for swellings and toothache, and to help overcome insomnia and treat digestive upsets. Native North Americans made tarragon tea to treat colds, diarrhea, dysentery, headache, and to assist women in childbirth. It is seldom used in modern medicine.
- Tarragon is rich in calcium and potassium, as well as vitamin A, thiamine, riboflavin, and niacin.

Dracunculus, in the herb's name, comes from the Latin draco, meaning "dragon." In the same vein, the English common name "tarragon" is a corruption of the French estragon, "little dragon," and is derived from the Arabic word for "dragon," tarkhun. The name may well come from tarragon's early reputation as a cure for snakebite. Indeed, Hippocrates, the renowned Greek physician, used tarragon to draw venom from snakebites and to alleviate the pain of bites from insects and mad dogs.

THYME, GARDEN *Thymus vulgaris*
Labiatae (Lamiaceae; mint family)

Also known as: Black thyme, common thyme, cooking thyme, English thyme, French thyme, German thyme, winter thyme

DESCRIPTION

- Garden thyme, just one of the more than 350 species of the genus *Thymus*, is an aromatic, shrubby perennial that grows from 15 to 50 cm (6 to 20 inches) tall. Believed to have been cultivated by the ancient Sumerians as long ago as 3000 BC, garden thyme continues to be the most popular culinary variety of thyme. It is a native of the European part of the western Mediterranean.
- Small, narrow, oval, dark green leaves are hairy underneath, with glistening oil glands on both surfaces, but particularly on the upper sides. The very fragrant leaves taste and smell warm, sharp, and bittersweet.
- Garden thyme has long, woody, branched stems, and sturdy roots.
- Produces loose whorls of lavender flowers clustered in "branchlets" or on rounded heads. Blooms in midsummer.
- May be grown in containers or pots, both outdoors and indoors.
- Flowers are rich in nectar and very attractive to honeybees.
- Leaves, stems, and flowers may all be eaten.

CULTIVATION NOTES

- Garden thyme prefers light, well-drained, slightly alkaline soil. Plants will not survive long in heavy, wet soil. Tolerated pH range is 4.5 to 8.0.
- Grows best in a sunny location where the plants are free from competition for light and room.
- Propagate garden thyme from seeds, stem cuttings, and layering.
- Plant seeds indoors about 8 to 10 weeks before your last frost date. Sow seeds to a depth of 6 mm (¼ inch) or less. Seeds germinate in about 2 weeks. Transplant the seedlings outdoors after the danger of frost has passed.
- Space plants 15 to 20 cm (6 to 8 inches) apart.
- Take stem cuttings in the spring. Clip a sprig of new growth from the top of the plant. Strip the leaves from the bottom of the twig and put it in wet sand to root.

Garden thyme

- Layer stems in late spring. Pin down the lower branches of an existing plant. Cover the branch with soil, leaving only the tip exposed. Once the pinned branch has rooted, remove it from the main plant. Thyme is a sprawling plant, so you may find that branches that reach over and touch the soil develop roots. This is a natural form of layering. When this occurs, separate off and transplant the new "plantlets."
- Divide mature plants every 2 to 3 years to prevent them from becoming woody and straggly.
- Susceptible to root rot and leaf spot, but usually pest-free.
- Overwinters outdoors up to zone 4. To provide winter protection, mulch well with straw or leaves. In regions north of zone 4, grow garden thyme as an annual.
- Pot outdoor plants for indoor use in fall. Indoor plants require at least 5 hours of strong direct sunlight daily. Add lime chips or coarse sand to regular potting soil to approximate the outdoor environment favored by garden thyme. Prune stem tips regularly to encourage bushy growth. Allow soil to dry between waterings.

> *The generic name Thymus comes from the Greek thumos, meaning "courage" or "strength." In ancient Greece, there was no higher compliment than to be told you smelled of thyme, a clear indication that your bravery was beyond question. The Greeks also believed that thyme could help overcome shyness. The association of thyme with courage lasted into the Middle Ages, when it was the custom for a lady to embroider a sprig of garden thyme on the scarf of her knight.*

HARVESTING NOTES

- Pinch off upper stems and strip leaves for fresh use as needed. Pick flowers as required.
- Harvest stems and leaves for drying just as flowering begins, cutting the entire plant back to about 5 cm (2 inches) above the ground. For the rest of the season, harvest only the tips of the branches so the plants are sturdy enough to survive fall and winter temperatures.
- To dry garden thyme, lay the stems flat or hang them in bunches in a shady, dry location. Strip the dried leaves from the stems and store in an airtight container.
- Freeze sprigs of garden thyme on a cookie tray and store in airtight freezer bags for use as required.

CULINARY USES

- Versatile garden thyme is indispensable in any kitchen. While it can be added fresh to various dishes, dried thyme with its penetrating sharper aroma is preferred by most cooks. Unlike many herbs, garden thyme, which is an essential ingredient of the classic French *bouquet garni*, does not lose its flavor when added early in the cooking process.
- Use thyme to season tomato sauces, seafood dishes, especially clams and mussels, and vegetables such as carrots, eggplant, onions, potatoes, peppers, and zucchini. Garden thyme complements clam and fish chowders, and mingles well with wine, onion, garlic, and brandy to flavor various meats, including sausages and roasts, wild game, and poultry, especially in recipes that specify long, slow cooking.

- Add fresh leaves and flowers to garden salads, and use the leaves, fresh or dried, to flavor butter and cooking oil.
- Brew a cup of refreshing thyme tea by infusing 15 mL (3 teaspoons) of crushed fresh leaves in 250 mL (1 cup) of boiling water. Cover and steep for 10 minutes, then strain the leaves. Sweeten with honey to taste.
- Garden thyme is used commercially to season olives, croutons, fried chicken, poultry stuffing mixes, and liver pâté. The essential oil of garden thyme is used to preserve processed meat and butter, and in making chewing gum, ice cream, candy, and the liqueur Benedictine.

> *The thymus gland, which is part of the human immune system, was so named by early anatomists because it reminded them of a thyme flower.*

CRAFT USES
- Include aromatic garden thyme in potpourris and sachets.

MEDICINAL USES
- In traditional folk medicine, garden thyme was used to treat anemia, asthma, bad breath, bronchitis, bruises, cancer, coughs and colds, colic, cramps, diabetes, diarrhea, fever, flatulence, gingivitis, gout, headache, indigestion, laryngitis, nerves, rheumatism, scarlet fever, snakebite, sprains, warts, whooping cough, and worms.
- Thyme oil has long been recognized as an antiseptic and disinfectant. The ancient Greeks, for example, used thyme to preserve fruits and wine inside wine vessels. Today, thyme oil is used in the pharmaceutical industry in antiseptic creams, mouthwashes, cough drops and cough syrups, and toothpaste.

> *According to Christian tradition, garden thyme was one of the herbs that lined the manger in which the infant Jesus lay. It is often included in modern Christmas nativity scenes.*

CAUTIONS
- Thyme oil may cause dermatitis in some people.
- Thyme oil should not be used for self-medication as it is poisonous. Thymol, which is found in thyme oil, can cause diarrhea, dizziness, headache, nausea, vomiting, muscular weakness, and can depress heart function, respiration, and body temperature.
- Thyme is reputed to affect the menstrual cycle, so taking it medicinally if you are pregnant or nursing is not recommended. Eating thyme while pregnant appears to be safe, however, as the amount normally consumed is less than medicinal doses.

CULTIVARS AND RELATIVES
Although most thymes can be propagated from seed, the desired flavor and aroma of seed-grown plants of many cultivars is unreliable. To avoid disappointment, buy plants from a reputable nursery, or obtain cuttings from existing plants.

In addition to the many varieties of upright thyme suitable for culinary use, there are several creeping varieties that make aromatic, colorful ground cover, even if their use in the kitchen is limited.

- Lemon thyme (*T. × citriodorus*). Rounded green leaves with pale purple or pink-mauve flowers. Develops into a compact, cushion shape. Grows 10 to 35 cm (4 to 14 inches) tall. Delicate lemon taste and bouquet are best when leaves are used fresh. Less hardy than garden thyme.
- Caraway thyme or seedcake thyme (*T. herba-barona*). Semi-prostrate, dwarf sub-shrub with arching branches, small, dark, shining leaves, and deep rose-pink flowers. Full-bodied flavor resembles thyme and caraway, but is more resinous. Use leaves fresh or dried. May be grown as an edible potted plant.
- Creeping thyme (*T. praecox, T. serpyllum*). Low, mat-forming thymes, generally no higher than 5 cm (2 inches), with rose-pink flowers. One form has a nutmeg scent and can be added to meat dishes or used as a pleasant tea.
- Lavender thyme (*T. thracicus*). Very pretty creeping variety forms thick, furry mats. Purple flowers have a strong lavender scent.
- Wooly thyme (*T. pseudolanuginosus*). Produces attractive mats of wooly gray leaves and dainty pale pink flowers. Has no scent or flavor, but contrasts beautifully with greener plants.

Since antiquity, thyme blossoms have been renowned for scenting the famous honey that comes from Mount Hymettus in Greece.

Nutmeg form of creeping thyme (T. praecox)

Carl Linnaeus (1707–1778), the great Swedish botanist and originator of the modern system of biological nomenclature, recommended an infusion of thyme to cure a hangover.

Warm-Season Container Herbs to Overwinter Indoors

BAY LAUREL
Laurus nobilis
Lauraceae (laurel family)

A native of western Asia Minor and perhaps parts of the European Mediterranean, this evergreen, broadleaf shrub can grow to 20 m (65 feet). Glossy, veined, stiff, spicy leaves are dark green on top and yellowish-green underneath, and are fragrant and sweet-scented with a lemon and clove over-tone. In spring, produces clusters of little, yellowish or greenish-white flowers, followed by dark purple or black berries. Buy plants from your local nursery or through a garden catalog. Grow in a tub filled with equal parts of sand, loam, and peat. Good drainage is essential. In winter, put tub in a sunny window. Water weekly with tepid water, but don't overwater. Apply slow-release fertilizer in November. Rotate tub every few days so that the sunlight reaches all sides evenly. Remove side shoots and suckers, and stake the plant to keep the trunk straight. Prune the top to a rounded shape, and repot when the root system becomes pot-bound. In spring, when all danger of frost is past, transfer tub outdoors to a sheltered, sunny loca-tion. When plant is actively growing, make sure the soil in the tub doesn't dry out. Leaves may be used fresh or dried. Taste intensifies through cooking, so add early in the preparation process. Remove leaves before serving. Bay is the primary taste of traditional French *bouquet garni*.

GINGER
Zingiber officinale
Zingiberaceae (ginger family)

Likely native to tropical Asia or Indonesia, ginger has
an underground thick, creeping, jointed, root-like stem, or
rhizome, that produces reed-like stalks 30 to 150 cm (1 to
5 feet) tall. Flowering stalks and non-flowering, leafy stems
emerge from the rhizome. (Ginger doesn't usually flower
in cultivation, but when it does, it produces
clusters of small purple blossoms in early spring.)
Edible ginger comes from the new growth of
rhizomes, which are tender and lack fibers. Plant rhizomes,
obtainable from your local grocery or through garden catalogs,
in a large pot of equal parts loam, sand, peat moss, and compost.
Place rhizomes horizontally 1 to 2 cm (½ to ¾ inch) deep
under the soil surface. (You can also cut the rhizomes into
smaller pieces, each with at least one "eye." This is best
done in spring as rhizomes are dormant during winter.) Keep
soil moist until new shoots appear, which may take more
than a month. Fertilize occasionally during the growing period. In winter, put pot in a sunny
window, although ginger will survive for many years even in an eastern- or western-facing
window. In spring, when all danger of frost is past, place pot outside in a sheltered, shady
location. Let plants grow for about 6 months before harvesting small portions of rhizome for
culinary use. Wash harvested rhizome and use immediately, or air-dry in the shade for a couple
of days before storing in an airtight container. Ginger has a distinctive, spicy, warm, aromatic
taste that rounds out the flavor of some foods, accents others, and contributes a unique freshness.

LEMON GRASS
Cymbopogon citratus
Gramineae (Poaceae; grass family)

Likely originated in India, Sri Lanka, or Indonesia, lemon grass
grows in thick, lemon-scented clumps or tufts 60 to 150 cm (2 to
5 feet) tall. The slightly enlarged, bulbous, juicy base is the most
edible portion. Produces small, greenish flowers at the top of the
stalks; however, cultivated plants rarely flower. Buy plants from
your local nursery or through a garden catalog. May also be
propagated by dividing existing clumps in spring or early
summer. To divide, simply tear sections from the base of the
mature plant. Before planting, cut leaves back to about 8 cm
(3 inches). Grow in a pot of well-drained but moisture-retentive

sandy loam. Keep well watered, but do not allow plant to become waterlogged. As clump grows, repot into successively larger containers. Indoor plants require as much sunlight as possible. In spring, when all danger of frost is past, transfer pot outside to a sheltered, sunny location. Lemon grass doesn't dry well, but it does keep in the refrigerator and freezer. Simply separate the lower basal portion from the upper, leafy part of the stem. Wrap both parts in foil and store in refrigerator. Stays fresh for about 2 weeks. Follow the same directions for freezing, only store in freezer bags. Use leaves and bulbous stems to brew fragrant tea, and to season Thai, Cambodian, and Vietnamese dishes, soups, tofu, vegetables, stir-fries, and calamari and shrimp dishes. Except for the young, tender, basal portions, lemon grass remains fibrous after cooking, and should be removed before serving.

LEMON VERBENA
Aloysia citriodora
Verbenaceae (vervain family)

Native to Chile, Argentina, Peru, and Uruguay, lemon verbena is a highly aromatic shrub that grows as tall as 5 m (16 feet) in mild climates and up to about 1 m (3 feet) when grown in pots. Narrow, pointed leaves grow in whorls of 3 or 4. Produces filmy spikes of small white and purple flowers in summer and autumn. Foliage has intriguing sharp, long-lasting, sweet lemon-lime flavor and fragrance. Buy plants from your local nursery or through a garden catalog. Grow in a mixture of equal parts of loam, sand, and leaf mold in a 30 cm (12 inch) container. Good drainage is essential. During the winter, keep indoor plants almost dry, and provide at least 5 or 6 hours of direct sunlight daily. In spring, when all danger of frost is past, transfer pots outdoors to a sheltered, sunny location. Keep moderately moist throughout the summer. When potted plants are brought back into the house before the first fall frost, they may lose their leaves. This is normal as lemon verbena is deciduous. In February, cut back plants to stimulate growth. Water sparingly, and keep cool until new growth appears. During active growth, keep the soil moist but not soggy. Repot in fresh soil mix every 2 to 3 years. Use leaves fresh, dried, or frozen. Fresh young leaves can be eaten like spinach. Leaves make a delicious tea, and can be used to flavor cold drinks, salads, dressings, fruit desserts, sauces, marinades, jellies, soups, omelettes, vegetables, fish, and meat dishes. As fresh leaves are tough, you should mince them finely if they are to be eaten rather than just used to impart flavor. Lemon verbena makes aromatic potpourris and sachets, and was the fragrance always associated with Scarlett O'Hara's mother in Margaret Mitchell's U.S. Civil War epic *Gone With the Wind*.

MYRTLE
Myrtus communis
Myrtaceae (myrtle family)

Native to the Mediterranean and northern Africa, myrtle is an attractive, evergreen bush. (Under the right growing conditions, myrtle is a tree that can grow up to 5 m (16 feet) tall.) Large, glossy, dark green leaves have a leathery texture and pointed tips. Produces white or pink-white flowers, followed by blue-black berries. Both leaves and berries have a spicy fragrance. Buy plants from your local nursery or through a garden catalog. May also be propagated from seeds, or by cuttings taken from young shoots in midsummer, or by layering. Grow in pots containing moderately fertile, well-drained, loam-based soil, enriched with leaf mold or other well-composted organic material. Tolerates low light and minimal watering during the winter. In spring, when all danger of frost is past, transfer pots outdoors to a sunny location. Repot plants every other year in early spring. When plants are actively growing, water well. Don't let the soil dry out or the plants will drop their leaves. Harvest leaves and flowers in late spring or early summer for drying. Leaves may be used fresh or dried. Dry berries and crush like pepper-corns before use. Use myrtle to flavor poultry, wild game, stuffing, sauces, wines, and liqueurs. Myrtle is a symbol of love and passion, so bridal bouquets often include a sprig. The richly aromatic dried flowers are prized in potpourris.

SOURCES

Here are some mail-order nurseries that specialize in herbs, or offer a particularly wide selection.

CANADA

Brackenstone Herbs
Box 752
Nelson, BC V1L 5R7

Country Green, Inc.
Box 356
Campbellville, ON N0B 2J0

Dominion Seed House
Box 2500
Georgetown, ON L7G 5L6

Early's Farm & Garden Centre Inc.
2615 Lorne Avenue
Saskatoon, SK S7J 0S5

Forget-me-Not Herbs
RR2
1920 Beach Road
Oxford Mills, ON K0G 1S0

Halifax Seed Company Inc.
Box 8026, Station A
5860 Kane Street
Halifax, NS B3K 5L8

The Herb Farm
RR 4
Norton, NB E0G 2N0

The Herb Garden
3840 Old Almonte Road
Almonte, ON K0A 1A0

Herbes du Verger
1600, chemin Ozias-Leduc
Mont-Saint-Hilaire, QC J3G 4S6

Herbs for all Seasons
RR 3
3383 8th Line Road
Metcalfe, ON K0A 2P0

Hole's Greenhouses & Garden Ltd.
101 Bellerose Drive
St. Albert, AB T8N 8N8

Island Seed Co.
Box 4278, Depot 3
Victoria, BC V8X 3X8

Lindenberg Seeds Ltd.
803 Princess Avenue
Brandon, MB R7A 0P5

McFayden Seed Co. Ltd.
30-9th Street
Brandon, MB R7A 6N4

Mycoflor Inc.
7850, chemin Stage
Stanstead, QC J0B 3E0

O'Kelly Herbes Médicinales
213, chemin Rocheleau
Sutton, QC J0E 2K0

Rawlinson Garden Seed
1979 Route 2 Highway
Sheffield, NB E3A 8H9

Richters
357 Highway 47
Goodwood, ON L0C 1A0

River View Herbs
Box 92
Highway 215
Maitland, Hants Co., NS B0N 1T0

Sage Garden Herbs
3410 St. Mary's Road
Winnipeg, MB R2N 4E2

Salt Spring Island Nursery
355A Blackburn Road
Salt Spring Island, BC V8K 2B8

Le Semences Solana
17, Place Léger
Repentigny, QC JA6 5N7

South Cove Nursery, Ltd.
Box 615
Yarmouth, NS B5A 4B6

Stokes Seeds Ltd.
Box 10
St. Catharines, ON L2R 6R6

T & T Seeds Ltd.
Box 1710
Winnipeg, MB R3C 3P6

Upper Canada Seeds
8 Royal Doulton Drive
Don Mills, ON M3A 1N4

Vesey's Seeds Ltd.
Box 9000
Charlottetown, PE C1A 8K6

West Coast Seeds
Unit 206
8475 Ontario Street
Vancouver, BC V5X 3E8

William Dam Seeds Ltd.
Box 8400
Dundas, ON L9H 6M1

UNITED STATES

Bluestone Perennials
7237 Midd le Ridge Road
Madison, OH 44057

Capriland's Herb Farm
534 Silver Street
Coventry, CT 06238

Circle Herb Farm
Route 1, Box 247
East Jordan, MI 49727

Clark's Greenhouse
Route 1, Box 15B
San Jose, IL 62682

Companion Plants
7247 N. Coolville Ridge Road
Athens, OH 45701

The Cook's Garden
PO Box 535
Londonderry, VT 05148

The Crownsville Nursery
PO Box 797
Crownsville, MD 21032

Forestfarm
990 Tetherow Road
Williams, OR 97544-9599

Fragrant Fields
128 Front Street
Dongola, IL 62926

Gilbertie's Herb Gardens
Sylvan Lane
Westport, CT 06880

Goodwin Creek Gardens
PO Box 83
Williams, OR 97544

The Gourmet Gardener
8650 College Boulevard
Overland Park, KS 66210

Greenfield Herb Garden
PO Box 9
Shipshewana, IN 46565

Hartman's Herb Farm
Old Dana Road
Barre, MA 01005

The Herb Garden
PO Box 773
Pilot Mountain, NC 27041-0773

The Herbfarm
32804 Issaquah-Fall City Road
Fall City, WA 98024

High Altitude Gardens
PO Box 1048
Hailey, ID 83333

J.L. Hudson, Seedsman
Star Route 2, Box 337
La Honda, CA 94020

Le Jardin du Gourmet
PO Box 75, Memorial Drive
St. Johnsbury Center, VT 05863

**Lewis Mountain Herbs
& Everlastings**
Route 247, 2345 Street
Manchester, OH 45144

Logee's Greenhouses
141 North Street
Danielson, CT 06239

Nichols Garden Nursery
1190 North Pacific Highway
Albany, OR 97321-4598

Park Seeds
Cokesbury Road
Greenwood, SC 29647-0001

Rasland Farm
Route 1, Box 65C
Goodwin, NC 28344-9712

The Rosemary House
120 South Market Street
Mechanicsburg, PA 17055

Sandy Mush Herb Nursery
316 Surrett Cove Road
Leicester, NC 28748

Shepherd's Garden Seeds
30 Irene Street
Torrington, CT 06790

Stokes Seeds, Inc.
Box 548
Buffalo, NY 14240

Sunnybrook Herb Farm
9448 Mayfield Road
Chesterland, OH 44026

Tinmouth Channel Farm
Box 428B, Town Highway 19
Tinmouth, VT 05773

Thompson & Morgan
PO Box 1306
Jackson, NY 08527

Well-Sweep Herb Farm
205 Mt. Bethel Road
Port Murray, NJ 07865

Westview Herb Farm
PO Box 3462
Poughkeepsie, NY 12603

Wrenwood Nursery
Route 4, Box 361
Berkeley Springs, WV 25411

FURTHER READING

Barash, Cathy Wilkinson, and Rosalind Creasy. *Edible Flowers: From Garden to Palate.* Golden, Colorado: Fulcrum Publishing, 1995.

Bennett, Jennifer. *The New Northern Gardener.* Buffalo, New York: Firefly Books (U.S.) Inc., 1996.

Blunt, Wilfred, and Sandra Raphael. *The Illustrated Herbal.* London, U.K.: Thames & Hudson, 1994.

Bremness, Lesley. *The Complete Book of Herbs.* New York, New York: Viking Studio Books, 1988.

Briccetti, Rebecca Atwater. *Cold Climate Gardening.* New York, New York: Houghton Mifflin Company, 2000.

Carr, Anna, et al. *Rodale's Illustrated Encyclopedia of Herbs.* Edited by Claire Kowalchik and William H. Hylton. Emmaus, Pennsylvania: Rodale Press, 1987.

Crockett, James Underwood, and editors. *Herbs.* (The Time-Life Encyclopedia of Gardening.) New York, New York: Time-Life Books, 1977.

DeBaggio, Thomas. *Growing Herbs: From Seed, Cutting, and Root.* Loveland, Colorado: Interweave Press, Inc., 1994.

Forsell, Mary. Heirloom *Herbs: Using Old-fashioned Herbs in Gardens, Recipes, and Decorations.* New York, New York: Random House, 1990.

Foster, Steven. *Herbal Renaissance: Growing, Using and Understanding Herbs in the Modern World.* Salt Lake City, Utah: Gibbs-Smith Publisher, 1993.

Gabriel, Ingrid. *Herb Identifier and Handbook.* New York, New York: Sterling Publishing, 1979.

Gardner, Jo Ann. *Living with Herbs.* Halifax, Nova Scotia: Nimbus Publishing Limited, 1997.

Gilbertie, Sal. *Kitchen Herbs: The Art and Enjoyment of Growing Herbs and Cooking with Them.* New York, New York: Bantam Books, 1988.

Head, William. *Gardening Under Cover: A Northwest Guide to Solar Greenhouses, Cold Frames, and Cloches.* Seattle, Washington: Sasquatch Books, 1989.

Heger, Mike, and John Whitman. *Growing Perennials in Cold Climates.* Chicago, Illinois: Contemporary Books, 1998.

Hemphill, John, and Rosemary Hemphill. *Herbs: Their Cultivation and Usage.* New York, New York: Sterling Publishing Company, 1984.

"Herbs and Cooking." *Brooklyn Botanic Garden Record.* Vol. 45, No.4, Winter 1990.

Hill, Lewis. *Cold-climate Gardening: How to Extend Your Growing Season by at Least 30 Days.* Pownal, Vermont: Storey Communications Inc., 1987.

Holt, Geraldine. *Recipes from a French Herb Garden.* London, U.K.: Corcoran Octopus, 2000.

Hopkinson, Patricia, Diane Miske, Jerry Parsons, and Holly Shimizu. *Herb Gardening.* New York, New York: Pantheon Books, 1994.

Lima, Patrick. *The Harrowsmith Illustrated Book of Herbs.* Camden East, Ontario: Camden House Publishing, 1986.

Lust, John. *The Herb Book.* New York, New York: Bantam Books, 1974.

Marcin, Marietta Marshall. *Herbal Tea Gardens.* Pownal, Vermont: Storey Books, 1999.

Mazza, Irma Goodrich. *Herbs for the Kitchen.* Boston, Massachusetts: Little, Brown and Company, 1976.

McClure, Susan. *The Herb Gardener.* Pownal, Vermont: Storey/Garden Way Publishing, 1996.

McIntyre, Anne. *The Medicinal Garden: How to Grow and Use Your Own Medicinal Herbs.* New York, New York: Henry Holt & Company, 1997.

Muenscher, Minnie. *Minnie Muenscher's Herb Cookbook.* Ithaca, New York: Cornell University Press, 1978.

Norman, Jill. *The Classic Herb Cookbook.* London, U.K.: DK Publishing, 1997.

Oster, Maggie, and Sal Gilbertie. *The Herbal Palate Cookbook.* Pownal, Vermont: Storey Publishing, 1996.

Perrin, Sandra. *Organic Gardening in Cold Climates.* Missoula, Montana: Mountain Press Publishing Co., 1991.

Phillips, Roger, and Martyn Rix. *The Random House Book of Herbs for Cooking.* New York, New York: Random House, 1998.

Phillips, Roger, and Nicky Foy. *The Random House Book of Herbs.* New York, New York: Random House, 1990.

Richardson, Noel. *Summer Delights: Cooking with Fresh Herbs.* 2nd edition. Vancouver, British Columbia: Whitecap Books, 1991.

Rinzler, Carol Ann. *The Complete Book of Herbs, Spices, and Condiments.* New York, New York: Facts on File, 1990.

Sands, Dave. *Herbs for Northern Gardeners.* Edmonton, Alberta: Lone Pine Publishing, 1992.

Sanecki, Kay. *The Complete Book of Herbs.* New York, New York: Macmillan, 1974.

Simmons, Adelma Grenier. *Herb Gardening in Five Seasons.* New York, New York: Plume, 1990.

Small, Ernest. *Culinary Herbs.* Ottawa, Canada: NRC Research Press, 1997.

Small, Ernest, and Paul M. Catling. *Canadian Medicinal Crops.* Ottawa, Canada: NRC Research Press, 1999.

Smith, Miranda. *Your Backyard Herb Garden.* Emmaus, Pennsylvania: Rodale Press, Inc., 1997.

INDEX

ABOUT THE AUTHORS

Dr. Ernest Small received a doctorate in plant evolution from the University of California at Los Angeles in 1969. He has authored more than 200 scientific publications on plants and has written 7 books. Two of his books, *Culinary Herbs* and *Vegetables of Canada,* won the Canadian Government's AgCellence Awards in 1998.

Grace Deutsch writes travel books and publishes educational resources. She grows herbs on her family's weekend farm in Bruce County, Ontario, not far from the cool breezes of Lake Huron.